10101010101
MICRO Series

101 COMPUTER PROJECTS FOR LIBRARIES

Patrick R. Dewey

American Library Association
Chicago and London
2000

While extensive effort has gone into ensuring the reliability of information appearing in this book, the publisher makes no warranty, express or implied, on the accuracy or reliability of the information, and does not assume and hereby disclaims any liability to any person for any loss or damage caused by errors or omissions in this publication.

Trademarked names appear in the text of this book. Rather than identify or insert a trademark symbol at the appearance of each name, the author and the American Library Association state that the names are used for editorial purposes exclusively, to the ultimate benefit of the owners of the trademarks. There is absolutely no intention of infringement on the rights of the trademark owners.

Project editor: Joan B. Grygel

Composition by Typographics Plus using Times and Helvetica typefaces

Printed on 50-pound white offset, a pH-neutral stock, and bound in 10-point coated cover stock by McNaughton & Gunn

The paper used in this publication meets the minimum requirements of American National Standard for Information Sciences—Permanence of Paper for Printed Library Materials, ANSI Z39.48-1992. ∞

Library of Congress Cataloging-in-Publication Data

Dewey, Patrick R., 1949–
    101 computer projects for libraries / Patrick R. Dewey.
        p. cm. — (101 micro series)
    Includes index.
    ISBN 0-8389-0772-5
    1. Libraries—United States—Data processing. I. Title.
  II. Title: One hundred one computer projects for libraries.
  III. Title: One hundred and one computer projects for libraries. IV. Series.
Z678.9.A4U625 1999
025´.00285—dc21   99-38371

Copyright © 2000 by the American Library Association. All rights reserved except those which may be granted by Sections 107 and 108 of the Copyright Revision Act of 1976.

Printed in the United States of America.

04 03 02 01 00   5 4 3 2 1

*This book is dedicated to the memory of
Mary T. Fletcher (1932–1999),
a good friend and coworker.
Mary, in charge of the Branch Library
of the Maywood Public Library for 18 years,
served her community with diligence,
dedication, and loyalty.
She will be missed.*

CONTENTS

PREFACE ix

Using Computers in Libraries 1

Administration: Budgeting, Accounting, and Record Keeping 6
    Annual Budgeting Process 6
    ARL Statistics 7
    Budgeting 8
    Central Library Recarpeting 8
    Congregational Records 9
    Copyright Compliance Files 11
    Tracking Miscellaneous Income 12

Bibliography Generation 13
    Triton College Video Catalog 13
    Videotape Bibliography Generation 14

Children, Young Adults, and Reading Club Projects 16
    Anguilla Library Computer Club 16
    After-School Computer Tutorial for Kids 17
    Computer Camp 18
    Family Computer-Literacy Grant 19
    Individual Research Project 20
    Totally Teen Book Talk 20
    Tots and Teens: Partners in Learning 21
    YA-Produced Videos 22
    Youth Access to Electronic Reference Sources 23

Circulation Systems and Online Catalogs 25
    Circulation and Cataloging in a University Library 25
    Circulation System in a Special Library 26
    Media-Booking Database 27

Online Catalog in a Corporate Library   27
Our Lady of Mount Carmel Parish Online Catalog   28
Sulzer Videotape Management System and Integrated Ordering System   29

Computer Centers and Labs   30
Law Library's Computer Labs   30
Library of the Health Sciences Twenty-Four-Hour Microcomputer Lab   32
Library Open-Access Computer Lab   32
Little Village Learning and Literacy Center   33
Mobile Public Online Computer Services (The MOBILE Project)   35
Portage-Cragin Branch Library Computer Center Building Program   36
Public Computer Labs   38
U.S. Navy Library Media Resource Center   38

Desktop Publishing and Graphics   40
Electronic Products Showcase: A Slide Show   40
Library News & Notes: An Electronic Newsletter for Faculty   41
Plainedge Public Library Program Newsletter   42
Production of *Library Links*: A Quarterly Newsletter   44

Indexing   45
Christian County Indexes   45
Electronic Index of Auto-Repair Manuals   46
Electronic Song Index   47
In-House Song Index   48
Local-Paper Obituary Index   49
Mel Tierney American Legion Post Digitization Project   49
Saskatchewan News Index   50

Interlibrary Loan   52
Coastal Bend Health Information Network   52
Web-Based Interlibrary Loan Forms   53

The Internet   54
Building Accessibility to Technology   55
Chicago Public Library Internet Access   56
Computer Tutors Put Vets on the Net   56
Developing an Internet Workshop Using a Class Home Page   57
Harvest Server   58
Kent County Library System Information Kiosk   59
Library Online Information Service (LOIS)   61

Contents   **vii**

    LIBSTATS: Library Statistics on the Web   62
    Park Ridge Community Network NorthStar: A North Suburban Library
        System NorthStarNet Project   63
    St. Joseph County Public Library Internet Use   64
    Scout Report for Science and Engineering, Scout Report for Business and
        Economics, Scout Report for Social Sciences   66
    Scout Report Research and Development   67
    Scout Report Signpost   69
    Staff and Patron Home Pages   70
    Statement of Internet Policy on Public Access PCs   71
    Treasure Island Web Site   71
    Using the Electric Library as an Information Resource
        in a Public Library   72

Local Area Networks, Intranets, and Cooperatives   74
    Developing and Planning a Local Area Network   74
    Network System's Securities   76
    Rochester Hills Public Library Staff Intranet   77
    Starkville High School Library Automation Consortium   78

Management   80
    Barcoding for Collection Analysis   80
    Library Activities Online Scheduling Project   81
    Materials Ordering Using B&T Link   82
    Monthly Report to the Library Board   83
    Payroll Using an Online Service   84
    Training-Center Schedule   85
    Using a Spreadsheet to Shift a Journal Collection   85
    Vitreous Proxy Server   86

Periodicals   88
    Electronic Magazine Routing   88
    North Carolina Periodicals Index   89

Public Access and Student and Patron Training   91
    Bibliographic Instruction   92
    Computer Literacy: A Multilingual Approach   93
    Digital Images from the American Radicalism Collection   94
    Introduction to Computers and the Internet   95
    Literacy Links: Adult Literacy/ESL Services   96

UMass Dartmouth

Meeting Training Demands through Videoconferencing 97
Online Bibliographic Instruction for Research and Library Use 97
Patron Training and Empowerment 98
Pilot Computer Training Center 99
Public Access Microcomputers at the Chicago Public Library 99
Public Computer Use for Word Processing and the Internet 101
Public Computer Workstations 101
Résumé Workshop at the Computer Center 103
White Rose IBM Computer Enthusiasts Library Club 105

Public Relations 106
　　The Library Cable Network: Public Relations through Cable Television 106
　　Portsmouth Computer Show 107

Reference 108
　　Client Tracking Conversion 108
　　Internet Web Site Index for Reference 109
　　Job-Search Resources Booklets 109
　　The Nuclear, Biological, and Chemical Terrorist Events CD-ROM 110
　　Public Inquiry Mail and Telephone Services Unit (PIMATS): Smithsonian Online 112
　　Reader's Advisory Resources Web Page 113
　　Regional Libraries for Access to Community Services (ReLACS) 114
　　Virtual Reference Librarian 116
　　Wall Charts for Reference 117

APPENDIXES

A Computer Periodicals of Interest 119
B Project Software 121
C Computer Software Companies 133

GLOSSARY 141

BIBLIOGRAPHY 149

INDEX 153

PREFACE

Almost every conceivable activity in a library has been automated—from staff scheduling to running a circulation system. This has been done both with simple machines of small capability and in large labs of many networked computers. A computer project is filled with problems and dangers. Most librarians who have introduced computers into their library for staff or public use can attest to this fact. The people who completed the 101 projects in this volume are no exception—they are some of the people who responded to the 3,500 questionnaires sent out to inquire about microcomputer use in libraries. Their information provided the basis for writing this book. The surveys were sent to people on various ALA mailing lists, Information Today's *Computers in Libraries* conference attendee mailing list, people selected from interesting Web sites, and many members of the Suburban Library System (Illinois) of which my own library, Maywood, is a part.

I wish to personally thank everyone who participated. It is not easy to find the time in today's busy library to fill out yet another questionnaire. The information in most project descriptions was compiled by the contact person for that project. All material was edited for conformity and style.

A lot has happened since the first edition of this volume was published in 1989: The Internet has taken the center stage in the world of computing. A simple PC can now connect anyone with vast libraries of information for research or other purposes, and it is possible to communicate with friends and colleagues around the world inexpensively using e-mail. Microcomputers have themselves become vastly more powerful and easy to use. Machine capabilities and add-ons can be purchased that were never dreamed of just a few years ago. In addition, very fast CD-ROM drives are now available. DVDs, new high-tech, massively large CDs, provide more space than most of us ever believed possible. Furthermore, an ocean of software is now increasingly intuitive. All of these hardware and software improvements and enhancements have made it easier to use a microcomputer for tasks and chores around the library that range from circulation systems to simple name-and-address files.

The next great wave of innovation in electronically assisted library services may be a vast improvement in disability accessibility. Print enhancement/enlargement systems are already commonly used in libraries. Voice recognition systems now allow an individual with limited sight or mobility to use many nonprint services. The great limiting factor has always been the expense and the great difficulty of using such devices. Their expense is decreasing, and their accuracy is increasing. For example, good voice recognition systems for word processing now cost only a few hundred dollars. Each one must, however, still be customized for the voice of each individual.

The projects in this book represent a wide cross section of the way microcomputers are used in libraries. They include school, special, public, and academic libraries. Some are single stand-alone projects while others are cooperative projects between different libraries or span a library system or even several countries.

These projects will supply those who read about them with new ideas for use at their own library. Most can be adapted with changes for the local environment.

Not covered in the previous edition of this book are the Internet projects and the "cybermobile." The cybermobile is used much like a bookmobile to send computers into local neighborhoods. The project in this book that used this technology was centered in Europe.

Major areas of computer use in libraries include public access for children and adults, administration, Internet access, classes, circulation, online catalogs, catalog search and request, report generation (with spell checkers and grammar-enhancement modules), public relations, computer rooms and labs, periodicals control, desktop publishing, and local area networks (with e-mail, Internet, printer, and CD-ROM sharing). All of these categories are represented in this book.

How to Use This Book

Reading about what others have undertaken in their libraries is an excellent way to begin to develop new ideas relevant to your own institution. This book is filled with success stories from all types of libraries: public, corporate, school, university, legal, etc. Most of the libraries included in this book have a contact person listed, along with e-mail address and fax number for follow-up questions.

For beginners, it is a good idea to take some workshops, especially about the use of specific high-level software packages such as WordPerfect or Microsoft Publisher. Visiting other libraries to see firsthand how they did what they did and to hear about their problems is also informative.

Use *101 Computer Projects* in conjunction with other tools and books. Other books in this series can be used to collect information about software, such as *303 Software Programs to Use in Your Library* and *303 CD-ROMs to Use in Your Library*. Included in the appendix is a bibliography for additional reading and a list of computer journals. The greatest access to information about software, however, is the Internet. Most software companies have Web sites with detailed information and contacts. Some educational sites have software review services and databases for finding software. Every effort has been made to include the program software in this book in appendix A. The manufacturers' addresses are listed in appendix B.

Readers of this book should experiment with microcomputer hardware and software. It is doubtful that we will ever leave the age of experimentation, since the computer is reinvented each year and is used differently by everyone who sits down at a keyboard. While few will be genuine pioneers, there are still new things that will bring greater efficiency and better service to the local community. Many of the projects in this book were experimental in nature.

Using Computers in Libraries

Being organized and informed with up-to-date information are perhaps the two most important personal ingredients for success when adding to or expanding microcomputer services. Unfortunately, all too often computers are purchased one at a time in response to an immediate demand or need. A better strategy is to think through the long-range and collective needs of the institution by developing a technology plan for the future. Such a plan can encompass tasks and areas to be affected, cost of equipment and software, installation, staff training, repair and replacement, and ergonomics.

There is an abundance of success stories in thousands of libraries, some of which are related in this book. How success is achieved is different in each library. Nevertheless, the basic steps necessary for success are fairly universal and serve as a useful guide. The first step is a conscious effort to learn more about the ever-changing world of technology.

Technology Plans

In virtually all areas involving computers in libraries, it is important for a library to have a technology plan. Such a plan is a rational way to organize for future change, and it can also be used as documentation when seeking grant monies. The first step toward a plan is needs identification. Although many libraries hire a consultant, it still pays to have a working knowledge of computers and software to be able to communicate intelligently with a consultant about hardware and software. The library's staff needs to recognize which services can best be aided with technology and which should be left alone.

A technology plan should look five years into the future and include a maintenance contract or upgrade schedule and a regular review process. It should be revised and updated yearly just as you do with your five-year plan. One source that can help you in this process is *Wired for the Future: Developing Your Library Technology Plan*.[1]

One important question to ask is how many workstations should be made available. Another is whether they should be networked or stand-alone. What are the advantages of networking? How many patrons will use the workstations? Once the doors have been opened, the public may rush in to use the equipment in large numbers. A general guide is to be as expandable and flexible as possible. Lots of money helps, too. In a new building, as many places as possible should be available for future computer use. Additional computers can be purchased to enlarge the network if it becomes necessary.

In most cases, it is necessary to have rules to provide for equitable computer use. For example, limiting computer use to one hour per day per patron will ration computer time. Putting the Internet on every computer can be a big mistake, since many high school computer users will show up to use the Internet and nothing else, monopolizing all available workstations. Such a situation can make it impossible for others to use any of the databases or application programs that may be available.

Software Selection

Software selection must be an ongoing process. Major packages may be purchased that provide library staff with state-of-the-art word processing, spreadsheets, and database management. Any of the major packages (for example, WordPerfect or Microsoft Word) will do the job. Some microcomputers come bundled with enough software for general use.

Library-specific software is another matter entirely. While the purchase of a single package to create catalog cards or route magazines may be left to the selection of a department or individual staff member, the purchase of an entire circulation or library system should be made by a team of library members, perhaps in consultation with other libraries that have already made such a purchase or with the aid of a consultant. Usually, the more sophisticated the software (that is, the more it does with more features), the more it costs. Most application programs can be purchased for different levels of sophistication.

Hardware Selection

Hardware selection can be difficult. Most libraries have gone with IBM or IBM clones, but some use Apple Macintosh computers or clones. There are some advantages to each approach. Deciding which platform to use is an individual decision based upon experience and knowledge of your unique work environment and situation.

Peripherals are also a major decision. They include hard drives, CD-ROM drives, scanners, monitors, printers, and components necessary to operate a local area network. Even keyboards and mice can be issues for selection (for example, do you need ergonomically correct keyboards and mice?). As you determine your needs, software, and the number of likely users, you can map out a selection of hardware.

The ultimate setup includes a local area network (LAN) that provides a lot of capability that a single PC or group of stand-alone PCs cannot. Especially important are CD-ROMs. On a LAN, any workstation can access CD-ROMs on a central tower or server. Workstations on a LAN can share e-mail, Internet connections, documents, printers, scanners, and hard disk space, if configured to do so. However, a LAN is also much more complicated than any single or group of stand-alone PCs, because a LAN requires more hardware and software. It also requires a separate closet or "computer room" where the servers reside. Furthermore, a LAN needs an employee with a great deal of technical sophistication to keep things going, to make improvements and install updates, and to fix things when they go wrong. The setup time and the "shakedown cruise" also take longer.

Elements of a Computer Project

The general elements of a computer project have remained the same in spite of technology changes over time. The planning-implementation-upgrade cycle has not changed. Following are five general steps for a computer project.

1. Identify all tasks or systems to be computerized (for example, making catalog cards).
2. Determine that these tasks need to be computerized as opposed to those that are better done manually.
3. Discuss computerization with staff, including the following questions:

    Who will be responsible for the equipment?

    Where will the equipment be housed?

    How will the staff be trained?

    How will expendables such as paper and ribbons be handled?

    How will equipment be repaired?
4. Decide how software will be selected. For example, one or two people can evaluate catalog card programs, but the entire staff should see at least some software demonstrated and arrive at a consensus on its applicability.

5. Determine what hardware is needed. Hardware selection should involve not only the computer brand but also the model, printer, drives, other accessories, and desk and ergonomic features (such as lighting, holders, etc.) that are necessary. Of course, this assumes that the computer hardware is not already owned by the library and in place.

The eight steps in planning and implementing computer technology follow. The actual steps that can be defined in the implementation process can rarely be followed in the exact order given here. Nevertheless, the first step for everyone should be the development of a technology plan following a consultation with experts. Nearly all libraries will have to budget for the purchase of equipment. While some libraries will already have the money, some will have to raise funds and some will receive grants. Planning ahead is crucial, since knowing how a computer can help to solve some problem or improve service is crucial.

An important element in sustaining any technology long term is a systematic review of the project including hardware, software, procedures, staffing, and maintenance. As time goes by, computers break down and software compatibility issues develop, and both become outdated. Early on in a computer's life span, it can make sense to upgrade it with memory, peripherals, and other hardware. Eventually, however, the CPUs themselves must be replaced.

1. A technology plan should encompass all of the areas of the library that might benefit from computer technology. Create individual plans for each department or each specific project. These plans should include the hardware, software, and staff to be involved.
2. Software areas of selection should include operating systems; library-specific, word processing, spreadsheet, and database management programs; browsers; and desktop publishing programs. Auxiliary or support programs should include virus protection, backup software, etc.
3. Hardware areas of selection should include the CPU, hard drives, modems, scanners, CD-ROM drives (including CD-Rs and DVDs), printers, memory, etc. LAN packages can include CD-ROM towers and routers.
4. Determine where all workstations will be located and who will use them. Make sure each workstation has adequate lighting. Develop rules for their use including appointments.
5. Some workstations, especially those that are networked, should be set up by the vendor. The vendor then takes responsibility if the programs don't work properly. A single or several PCs may be set up by library staff, assuming they have adequate expertise.
6. It is essential to give staff adequate time and workshops to train. Many local community colleges and high schools provide day and evening workshops on the use and repair of computers and on the use of major applica-

tions packages, such as WordPerfect or Quattro Pro. Once everything has been installed, simply getting the professional staff together to explain the databases and their use will be a big help. Some libraries attempt some instruction for the public. Bringing in outside teachers is often the best solution for application training.

7. After applications packages have been installed, it is necessary to regularly upgrade programs. Most libraries need to change or upgrade some component soon after a system is installed. The computer world is a difficult one with which to keep up. On the Internet there are many "patches" (fixes) and updates for programs. Virus-detection programs also require regular updates to keep current so they can trap ever-evolving computer viruses.

8. Feedback should be a part of every project. This means regularly inspecting the project or communicating with staff involved. Needs change, as does the world.

NOTE

1. Diane Mayo and Sandra Nelson, *Wired for the Future: Developing Your Library Technology Plan* (Chicago: American Library Assn., 1999).

Administration:

Budgeting, Accounting, and Record Keeping

Many administrative tasks can be improved with the aid of a microcomputer. Most library directors with access to a PC already use a spreadsheet to make the budgeting process more efficient and accurate. Tailoring budget categories to fit within a specific income can be done in a very short time since revisions can be made over and over instantly. The spreadsheet is the "what if?" software that is so very popular with accountants and administrators. Charts and other graphic elements can point out where the money is going in a way that is not possible with just raw data.

A payroll system can be improved by using the microcomputer and modem to send the necessary information to the agency responsible for writing checks. One unusual project in this chapter is the use of a computer to make calculations necessary to recarpet a library, undertaken by the Kitsap Regional Library.

Database programs are used by many libraries to maintain record files of all types. Congregational records are kept organized by the Presbyterian Church (USA) using a PC-File database. This includes a history of the church and other information. Other uses documented in this chapter include tracking miscellaneous expenses and tracking copyright compliance. Dozens of other administrative uses for a microcomputer can be found by just applying the spreadsheet, database management system, or word processing to simple everyday tasks that will make life easier.

Name:	**Annual Budgeting Process**
Library:	Maywood Public Library
Contact:	Patrick R. Dewey, director
Address:	121 S. Fifth Ave., Maywood, IL 60153
Phone:	(708) 343-1847; Fax: (708) 343-2115
E-mail:	patrickdewey@hotmail.com
Hardware:	IBM PC
Software:	Microsoft Works, Quattro Pro

Administration: Budgeting, Accounting, and Record Keeping **7**

Description: Microsoft Works has been used for years at the Maywood Public Library to calculate the annual budget, although any spreadsheet would do as well. The library recently converted to Quattro Pro because of its additional flexibility and its integration with WordPerfect, of which it is a component.

The library uses two spreadsheets: one for income and another for expenses. The first step was to set up the income sheet. In the first column labels for each source of anticipated revenue were entered into the spreadsheet as well as a total. A second spreadsheet was similarly set up with budget categories in the first column (such as salaries, books, videotapes, etc.). Additional columns to the right were labeled previous year, present year, and percentage of total along with their totals at the bottom. By inserting the anticipated budget amounts, it was possible to tell whether the two spreadsheet totals (income and expenditures) matched. The total budget could not exceed the total amount listed for income.

Items may be cut and pasted anywhere, making it easy to revise. The spreadsheets can be expanded to include additional sources of revenue or budget categories. During the process, amounts in the budget categories can be easily changed ("what if?"). A comparison can also be made between this year's and last year's totals. The spreadsheet arrangement also makes it easy to see the percentage of budget each item represents.

Once an acceptable budget has been achieved, it is printed out for use by the library board at its budget meeting. The board especially likes the percentage column since it allows spending comparisons across categories. A multiple-year budget, including the next five years for advanced planning, can be created to help foresee potential problems. The formulas should be kept as simple as possible.

Project length: 1992–present
Cost: None; preexisting microcomputer and software were used

Name: **ARL Statistics**
Library: Association of Research Libraries
Contact: Julia Blixrud, senior program officer
Address: 21 Dupont Circle, Washington, DC 20036-1118
Phone: (202) 296-2296; Fax: (202) 872-0884
E-mail: jblix@arl.org
Hardware: PCs and Macs
Software: SPSS, Microsoft Excel

8   Administration: Budgeting, Accounting, and Record Keeping

Description:	A survey form collects data over a Web site; the raw data results are run through sets of statistical programs. Results are tabulated and compiled into a printed publication, and data are also available electronically.
References:	http://www.arl.org/stats/
	Also, see *ARL Statistics*, an annual publication.
Project length:	Ongoing

Name:	**Budgeting**
Library:	Glenside Public Library District
Contact:	Michael Moulds
Address:	25 E. Fullerton Ave., Glendale Heights, IL 60139
Phone:	(630) 260-1550; Fax: (630) 260-1433
Hardware:	Compaq USA PC
Software:	Microsoft Excel
Description:	To more efficiently maintain information about departmental expenses, a spreadsheet with the date of purchase, order number, vendor's name, amount encumbered, amount billed, and credits was created using Microsoft Excel. The result was an easy-to-control departmental expenditure spreadsheet, independent from the monthly treasurer's report, that lists billed amounts in total for the month and for year-to-date. All materials expenditure information is entered on a regular basis, including expenditures for books, videotapes, audiotapes, CDs, etc.
	With the tabulated information, staff can track how much money is left in the materials budget. The spreadsheet calculates actual billed prices instead of just the encumbered amounts. The printout also assists staff in knowing at a glance which books and materials are on order. This was an easy project to conceive and put into practice. There have been no problems.
Project length:	1996–present
Cost:	None

Name:	**Central Library Recarpeting**
Library:	Kitsap Regional Library
Contact:	Sandy Carlson
Address:	1301 Sylvan Way, Bremerton, WA 98310
Phone:	(360) 405-9111
E-mail:	sandy@linknet.kitsap.lib.wa.us
Hardware:	US Micro Pentium PC
Software:	Microsoft Word 6.0, Microsoft Windows for Workgroups 3.1

Description:	The central branch has a 25,000-square-foot public area with an additional 10,000 square feet of space for a system that supports the library district, and a new carpet was long overdue. In 1997, the central library was carpeted and remodeled, and all furniture and book stacks were rearranged. Advantage was taken of the work to fix the concrete floor and rearrange both public and work areas in a more efficient way. Although the services of an architectural team were used to rearrange the public area (the staff area was done by staff), the cost of a furniture inventory was saved by doing the work internally. Using word processing tables, the staff identified, numbered, and labeled all furniture, book stacks, and other materials. The files were then manipulated according to the need to produce printed documents appropriate for each stage of the operation.

The first document was paired with a notebook of photographs and used by the design team to determine new locations for the items. The files were next used to identify items to be discarded or replaced. Later the files were used to identify where things were to be stored or used during the time the library was closed. Finally they were used with the project drawings to identify new locations as staff and volunteers returned items to the buildings.

Each piece of furniture was given a number that was entered into the table. Pertinent information on each piece was entered in the appropriate column. Columns included number, quantity, room location, type, dimensions, condition, uses, and comments. In the public area, identical furniture pieces were given the same number, but in the staff area each piece had a unique number so that the correct pieces would be returned to the right person. Using the database, sticky labels were printed to place on the items. More than 600 separate items were tracked and sorted through the nine months of the project.

Shelving was identified by type, height, and depth. The exact number of uprights, backs, tops, and bases was known. This made it possible to easily determine if there were enough pieces for the new layout.

Project length:	January 2, 1997–September 15, 1997

Name:	**Congregational Records**
Library:	Presbyterian Church USA (Department of History)
Contact:	Richard Bater, manager of research services
Address:	425 Lombard St., Philadelphia, PA 19147-1516
Phone:	(215) 627-1852; Fax: (215) 627-0509

E-mail:	rbater@hslc.org.
Hardware:	IBM PC compatible
Software:	PC-File 5 (shareware dBase clone)
Description:	The Department of History is the National Archives and Historical Research Center of the Presbyterian Church (USA). It is headquartered in Philadelphia with a regional office in Montreat, North Carolina, and a records management program at the denomination's headquarters in Louisville, Kentucky. The department serves the administrative, legal, and historical needs of the church's national agencies, middle governing bodies, and local congregations as well as scholars and the general public. It houses the official records of the denomination and its predecessor denominations, personal papers of prominent Presbyterians, the records of ecumenical organizations such as the American Sunday School Union and the National Council of Churches of Christ, and special collections and rare books supporting research in Presbyterian history. Collection emphases include church legal and administrative decisions; religion and life in Colonial America, the American Revolution, and the First and Second Great Awakenings; missionary work among Asians, Africans, and Native Americans; the New Republic; the Civil War and Reconstruction; westward expansion; civil rights and other race issues; social justice issues; and ecumenical movements.

To assist in this work, a computerized database was created using PC-File 5, a program similar in nature to dBase. Separate fields included the location of the holding, the name of the holding library, the name of the church, the date of the document, a description, and a scope (folder) designation. The system was designed and is managed by Richard Bater with the help of a technical services assistant. It was easy to set up.

Eight thousand vertical file folders were originally input into the system; more are added regularly. It has been a wonderfully useful system, since the library gets requests for the information contained in the folders on a daily basis from libraries and churches around the country. The database cuts down the amount of time it takes to locate information.

PC-File 5 is used to create a flat ASCII (.dbf) text file that is to be used for MARC conversion. The system is available online on a CD-ROM as part of the library catalog. |
| Project length: | June 1998–December 31, 1998 |
| Cost: | Internally funded |

Name:	**Copyright Compliance Files**
Library:	Covington & Burling Library
Contact:	Lawrence S. Guthrie II
Address:	Covington & Burling Library, 1201 Pennsylvania Ave. NW, Washington, DC 20004
Phone:	(202) 662-6158
E-mail:	LGUTHRIE@COV.COM
Hardware:	IBM compatible
Software:	WordPerfect
Description:	In an academic, public, or other not-for-profit library, the U.S. Copyright Guidelines dictate that the use of five articles from one journal title per year is permissible. Once the borrowing of five articles with no charge under fair use is exceeded, the royalties must be paid for the copying of subsequent articles during the year, or permission must be obtained from the copyright holder to make any further copies.

To monitor the use of these articles, a WordPerfect file was set up. Each requested and received interlibrary loan document is entered into this file. The entry begins with exact journal title, the volume, number, pages, article title, and the patron for whom it was ordered. The next time an article is requested and obtained, it is entered into the file by finding the alphabetical location of the journal title and entering it after any other entries of the same title.

It is very necessary to count when the five fair-use articles have been exhausted by finding the alphabetical location of the title before entering. Once the limit has been exceeded, the interlibrary loan librarian tries to obtain permission to make another copy or arranges to pay the royalties directly to the publisher or copyright holder or through the CCC to be in compliance with the Copyright Guidelines.

References:	Mary E. Jackson, "Library to Library: Copyright and ILL," *Wilson Library Bulletin* 66 (Dec. 1991): 84.
	Lawrence S. Guthrie II, "Copyright and Document Delivery," *Information Outlook* 1 (Jan. 1997): 39.
	http://www.fairuse.stanford.edu
Project length:	Ongoing
Cost:	None

Name:	**Tracking Miscellaneous Income**
Library:	Klinck Memorial Library, Concordia University
Contact:	Kristin Flanders
Address:	7400 Augusta St., River Forest, IL 60305
Phone:	(708) 209-3057
E-mail:	CREFLANDERS@crfcuis.edu
Hardware:	IBM PC compatible
Software:	Quicken
Description:	The goal of this project was to provide an easy accounting system for miscellaneous library income such as fines, printer charges, lost book receipts, ILL receipts, fax receipts, book sale receipts, and fiche duplication receipts. These had previously been manually stored in a paper ledger and then transcribed to a spreadsheet—a duplication of effort—and the spreadsheet was considered an unwieldy tool. Using Quicken it was easy to set up and customize fields for each separate income item. Information is entered into the system on a daily basis. A report can be made for any field. Quicken was a good selection because several staff members already had experience using it.
Project length:	1996–present

Bibliography Generation

Most librarians publish bibliographies of useful titles, including new books and other media owned by the library. These serve as a way to inform and update patrons. Most database systems or word processing systems can be used to do the job. Triton College maintains a list of videotapes on a special bibliographic software package designed with librarians in mind called ProCite. A word processor such as WordPerfect can be used to set up a file that can be sorted by any word position in the line of a document or by paragraph. This is a function much like that of a database system. Systems such as ProCite for Windows or Visual Fox-Pro can be used to create even more sophisticated bibliographies because they allow great control over data.

Name: **Triton College Video Catalog**
Library: Triton College Library/LRC
Contact: Lucy Smith
Address: 2000 Fifth Ave., River Grove, IL 60171
Phone: (708) 456-0300 x3747
E-mail: lsmith@triton.cc.il.us
Hardware: IBM PC 486
Software: ProCite for Windows
Description: The objective of this project was to create a printed catalog of the library's videotape collection including a subject index, to develop a continuing database of current items to print as supplements to the catalog, and to be able to search this database electronically on the local area network or through the library's Web site.

First, staff created a complete inventory of all of Triton's videotapes. Subject headings were determined and assigned for each title, and the database was customized with local notes. Each title was given an in-house accession number, the standard bibliographic description, and LC call number and classification. The first printed catalog was arranged by title and included some 1,500 records and 750 subject headings. New or deleted titles are updated on a regular basis.

At present, librarians are able to search the database through the local area network, though not yet on the Web. Some of the problems encountered were problems with ProCite that had to be overcome. Also, the database became too large to back up properly. It is recommended that an adequate backup copy of the database be made with a Zip drive or Zip disc to handle the large database size. Good planning is also recommended, including written rules and guidelines to streamline the input process for consistency and simplification.

Project length: Ongoing

Name:	**Videotape Bibliography Generation**
Library:	Maywood Public Library
Contact:	Patrick R. Dewey, director
Address:	121 S. Fifth Ave., Maywood, IL 60153
Phone:	(708) 343-1847; Fax: (708) 343-2115
E-mail:	patrickdewey@hotmail.com
Hardware:	IBM PC compatible, 16 MB RAM, Hewlett Packard LaserJet 4+ printer
Software:	WordPerfect 7
Description:	Though time-consuming, this project was worth the effort. The videotape collection currently consists of about 4,000 videotapes. While these are in the online catalog, most people do not want to look through the online system to find a videotape; instead, they browse. Tapes are arranged in their original boxes on open stacks, much like in a videotape rental store, and are arranged alphabetically within categories. They are tagged with security strips for protection.

Many patrons, however, ask for a specific tape by title, so a paper title list of all tapes is also available. Tapes on the list are identified by a corresponding subject category. The patron then goes to the shelf and locates the tape within that category by title. Using the database function of WordPerfect, the list was created using only two fields. The first field is for category (for example, horror, how-to, etc.); the second field is for the title. Once data has been entered, it may be sorted by either field. In this way, the database management functions are available through the word processor. The list is then printed out by category and by title, and copies are kept in the videotape department. The list could be searched electronically, but at present no computer is available in the videotape area.

There have been a few problems with the sort process, but none proved very difficult. The major problem was training staff to use the sort function. Some items, such as numbers, do not sort alphabetically as if spelled out. If necessary, these can be entered manually using the word processing function. Sometimes, videotape titles are longer than can be accommodated by the printed list (which is printed out two columns per page). In such cases, unwanted word wraps result; these must be changed manually.

Smaller collections, such as CD-ROMs and audio CDs, have also been similarly processed. Processing the talking books collection is a future project.

The original lists were input by the AV staff. All new materials are now input by the technical services staff prior to the materials being shelved.

Project length: 1992–present
Cost: Preexisting hardware and software in technical services department; no additional cost except staff time

Children, Young Adults, and Reading Club Projects

Represented in this chapter are many exciting projects to serve young people of all ages. These include teen programs, programs for small children, and programs for the whole family. Literacy programs are also popular at many libraries, since computer software is available for teaching people how to read. The Anguilla Library Computer Club on the Internet teaches young people basic computer skills, word processing, and other subjects. This project shows what can be done if the staff is determined to succeed. Computer Camp at the Roanoke County Public Library is a four-week spring program involving both children and their parents. The Totally Teen Book Talk program uses a database prepared by the library staff to recommend books to young people. Other than the preparation of reviews, it involves no additional staff time. The young adults at the Eisenhower Public Library used the library's equipment and computers to produce two videotapes about the library.

Name: **Anguilla Library Computer Club**
Library: Anguilla Library
Address: Anguilla Computes, Global Links, 4809 Penn Ave., Pittsburgh, PA 15224
E-mail: axanat@mail.candw.com.ai
Hardware: 640 K IBM PC with color monitor and 2 floppy disk drives; scanners; a digital camera
Software: Variety of educational titles such as School Mom, Googol Math Games, Typing Made Easy, and Adventure; Microsoft Windows
Description: The island of Anguilla, a British dependency, is one of the leeward islands in the West Indies, east of Puerto Rico. The people running this program are proud of their work that makes computer technology and educational software available to students who might otherwise miss out on both. The program is an excellent example of how to get maximum use out of just a few computers,

even if they are not the most recent models. It is significant to note that none of these computers has a mouse, CD-ROM, sound card, high resolution graphics, hard drive, etc. Computers have been donated from a variety of local and distant sources. The computer club, in fact, began with seven "ancient computers."

A series of Internet classes or lessons for achieving computer literacy introduce students to computers, teach them how to use a disk and how to boot a computer, and provide step-by-step instructions for using each program. All software must be available on a 360 K diskette and use CGA graphics. The program is limited to using software written prior to 1994. Nevertheless, it also uses the Internet to find programs. The library also invites donations of older software. Software training includes Windows, spreadsheets (including macros), and various applications. The original game of Adventure is also popular with the club because it will play on any of the older machines. Hardware training consists of teaching the basics of turning a computer on and off, opening and closing its case, identifying its parts, the proper handling of disks, installation of cards, CD-ROM drives, and motherboards.

The library's Web site at http://www.offshore.com.ai. computerclub/ has a list of lessons from other sources that provide more resources and opportunities for learning. The computer club is located in its own room. It holds regular meetings on Mondays from 4 to 6 P.M. for adults age 15 years and older and on Thursdays after school from 3:30 to 5 for those age 14 years and younger.

Project length: Ongoing

Name: **After-School Computer Tutorial for Kids**
Library: Roden Branch, Chicago Public Library
Contact: Bruce Fox
Address: 6083 N. Northwest Hwy., Chicago, IL 60639
Phone: (312) 744-1478
E-mail: bfox@chipublic.org
Hardware: Gateway P100 with color monitor and printer
Software: Microsoft Windows, Microsoft Word, Microsoft Publisher
Description: This after-school class, held twice weekly, tutors young children in the use of computers. While there have been few problems, it is recommended that the group size be kept small. Classes have five students and last for 45 minutes. The lessons, taught by the children's librarian, consist of an introduction to computers, get-

ting around Windows with a mouse, writing a basic document, printing, and a few advanced features. The tutor attempts to remain flexible with the subject matter. Classes are tailored to each individual group. Many of the participants have access to their own home computer.

Project length: Ongoing

Name: **Computer Camp**
Library: Roanoke County Public Library System
Contact: Jay Stephens
Address: 3131 Electric Rd., Roanoke, VA 24018
Phone: (540) 772-7507
E-mail: jstephen@vsla.edu
Hardware: Gateway PCs and printers, overhead with an LCD pad
Software: Netscape Navigator, various games on CD-ROM
Description: The Roanoke County Public Library System first introduced public Internet access in the spring of 1996. The library's first Internet training class for the public took place during the summer of that same year. The second annual Computer Camp was completed in the summer of 1998. Computer Camp was conceived of as an opportunity for children to receive personal instruction and hands-on experience with computers and the Internet. Over a two-week period (four sessions), 80 children learn how a computer works, how to hook one up, what the Internet is and how to use it safely, how to use search engines, how CD-ROMs and DVDs work, and much more. All of the instruction at Computer Camp is provided by members of the library's staff.

Camp usually runs two hours each day, and campers can choose morning or afternoon sessions. Snacks are provided for the campers, as are computer disks, handouts, and free printouts. At the end of camp there is a graduation ceremony at which the children receive certificates.

Both children and parents fill out surveys at the end of Computer Camp. Answers on both sets of surveys have been consistently positive and indicate that the children enjoy the camp and that parents are glad that the library offers the program. For only $10, a child receives several hours of personal instruction, food, and materials and gets to have fun and make new friends. Parents know that Computer Camp is a great bargain.

Above all else, a program like Computer Camp needs to be fun. It cannot simply mirror a school classroom. Camp instructors must present the material in a way that allows the children to get excited about it. A relaxed atmosphere and competent instructors who enjoy teaching provide a recipe for a successful camp.

No major problems have been encountered. One minor occasional problem is with parents who are late picking up their children. The instructors have to wait for the parents to arrive. As the instructors are members of the library's staff, they often have other duties to attend to and need to leave soon after a camp session has ended.

Reference: http://www.co.roanoke.va.us/library/
Project length: Spring 1996–present

Name: **Family Computer-Literacy Grant**
Library: Montague Branch, Rockford Public Library
Contact: Ivonne Spelman
Address: 215 N. Wyman St., Rockford, IL 61101-1023
Phone: (815) 965-6731
E-mail: ivonne@Arockford.lib.il.us
Hardware: IBM PC compatibles
Software: Microsoft Windows; A to Zap!; Fun with a Purpose; Living Books, Lib. 1; Magic School Bus; Human Body; Millie's Math House; My First Amazing; World Explorer; Read for Meaning; Sammy's Science House
Description: This project's goal was to provide educational software on CD-ROMs to enable parents and their children to improve reading, math, writing, and thinking skills. Since parents are the first teachers a child knows and are the most important allies of school and library educators, the goal was to support family literacy training. The program focused on "at risk" families—families with low basic skills or whose primary language was not English—those least likely to have access to computers. Libraries provide the space, equipment, and staffing. In this project strong cooperation existed between the library and the Rockford Public School District. Through the Title 1 program, "at risk" parents were identified.

The state grant offering provided the software. Families met every Saturday from 10 A.M. to 1 P.M. from November 1997 to May 1998. Spanish language students from a nearby high school were recruited to help both with the software and basic communications. A final report was prepared. An application for a second grant offering has been submitted.

Project length: November 1997–May 1998
Cost: The grant funding is an integral part of the Secretary of State Literacy Office program Educate and Automate. The grant offered approximately $500 in software and paid for 2 Rockford Public Schools instructors.

Name: **Individual Research Project**
Library: New Eagle Elementary Library
Contact: Lee Dastur
Address: 507 Pugh Rd., Wayne, PA 19087
Phone: (610) 688-0246
E-mail: DasturE@TESD.K12.A.US
Hardware: 5 Power Macintosh computers
Software: Computerized encyclopedias (Golden Book, Encarta), Microsoft's Dangerous Animals, computerized library database (Library 4), Netscape Navigator (particularly Yahooligans), and various CD-ROMs
Description: This project was conducted with fourth graders, the "seniors" at the New Eagle Elementary School. Previous years' library activities had been directed at how to use CDs, Netscape Navigator, the computerized library database, etc. Students were asked to select any topic that they would like to learn more about. They would then research it using all means at their disposal, compile their findings, and present a five-minute talk, with visuals, to the class.

Notable difficulties with the project related to note taking—what to leave in and what to take out. In many cases, there was an avalanche of material available, so sorting through it became difficult. In a few cases, little information was available. Notable successes related to student enthusiasm, which was very high, and to improvements in individual work habits. The entire project is viewed as the culmination of years of skill-building involving information retrieval, analysis and interpretation of data, and creation of original documents.
Project length: March 1, 1998–June 1, 1998

Name: **Totally Teen Book Talk**
Library: Orland Park Public Library
Contacts: Mary Weimar and Mary Adamowski
Address: 14760 Park Lane, Orland Park, IL 60462
Phone: (708) 349-8138
E-mail: ADAMOWSM@SLS.LIB.IL.US

Hardware:	IBM PC compatible
Software:	WordPerfect
Description:	Young adults in grades six and above are an interesting group of patrons. They enjoy reading, but they do not relish entering a library and being "pounced" upon by a librarian offering assistance. They would rather inconspicuously blend into the stacks, grab a book, and then run for the door. With this understanding, and the fact that it is important not to lose this precious audience, a painless, fun way was devised to select fiction reading material.

Staff from the youth services department select and read a young adult novel. They then write a short summary that includes the title, author, genre, grade level, and the number of pages. A short summary of the book is then written in book-talk form as if the staff were speaking directly to the reader. Just enough detail is given to entice the reader without giving the librarian's opinion of the book. The book talk is then input on a PC, printed, and mounted on a 4 × 6 sheet of colorful construction paper. After it has been laminated, a hole is punched in the upper corner, and it is attached to a ring hook. To make reading selection easier, the book talks are divided into different genres.

The library staff takes great pride in seeing a young adult flip through the book talks and then check out a selection. It has been a very successful program. The staff looks forward to continuing and improving it.

Project length:	Ongoing

Name:	**Tots and Teens: Partners in Learning**
Library:	Tinley Park Public Library
Contact:	Mary Lou Seery, youth services librarian
Address:	17101 S. 71st Ave., Tinley Park, IL 60477
Phone:	(708) 532-0160
E-mail:	seerym@sublibsy.sls.lib.il.us
Hardware:	4 Compaq PCs with dual headphones connected via a LAN
Software:	Curious George, Winnie the Pooh and the Honey Tree, Peter Rabbit, Just Grandma and Me, The Tortoise and the Hare, Dr. Seuss's ABCs
Description:	As originally conceived, twelve parent/child pairs were signed up for six weeks. Each session lasted one hour and was divided into twenty-minute segments. Parents and children would rotate between segments, which included computer time, time for introducing the author and his/her works, and an activity session. Groups were rotated weekly so that each group got a chance to

be on the computers first. A Youth Services Librarian was in charge of each program, and another librarian was available to help with the computers.

It quickly became apparent that both parents and children were anxious to have more computer time. In the second group of six weeks, the format was changed slightly to eliminate the activity portion of the program, thereby expanding computer use but still incorporating the program-related literature. This worked much better. However, in subsequent months it was decided to limit the participation to four parent/child groups and run each session for three weeks to give each group a half-hour with each software program. This was a still more favorable arrangement. The introduction to literature was maintained to keep the program library related.

The program is intended to run again this year with a further refinement. Four parent/child pairs will be signed up each week, allowing them to use the computers as they see fit but maintaining the display of literature and the availability of library staff for assistance.

Staff input was originally heavy. However, it lessened as staff and patrons became familiar with the computers and software.

It would definitely be worth doing again, as it has enabled a large number of patrons to become familiar with computers, children's software, and some authors they may not have known before. Parents were enthusiastic about the program.

Project length: September–December 1997
Cost: $1600, including cost of hardware and desks, funded through an Illinois State Library LTA grant

Name: **YA-Produced Videos**
Library: Eisenhower Public Library
Contact: Penny Blubaugh
Address: 4652 N. Olcott, Harwood Heights, IL 60646
Phone: (708) 867-7828
E-mail: blubaugh@sls.lib.il.us
Hardware: PC and Macintosh, Macintosh scanner, various printers
Software: Microsoft Word, MacGraphics Interface
Description: A young adult group produced two library-related videotapes. A copy of each was given to area schools, and multiple copies were retained at the library for checkout.

To produce the videos, the participants created scripts using the word processing program Microsoft Word. They created covers on Macintosh computers using scanners. Video footage was shot, mixed, and cut at Ridgewood High School and on location at the library as a local history video. The two titles were "Live! (On tape) at the Library" and "A Tale of Two Ridges." These were also shown several times on public access TV stations.

One of the problems encountered was the antiquated editing equipment that was available. Newer equipment now available will make this less of a problem if more videos are shot in the future.

Project length: Each video took approximately three months to produce in 1998

Name: **Youth Access to Electronic Reference Sources**
Library: Rockford Public Library
Contact: Andrew Finkbeiner
Address: 215 N. Wyman St., Rockford, IL 61101
Phone: (815) 965-6732
E-mail: andrew@rockford.lib.il.us
Hardware: *Workstations:* Pentium 100 processor, 1.2 GB hard drive, 16 MB RAM, 256 color monitor, 1 MB video card, Hewlett Packard laser printer
Server: Microtest optical storage and retrieval system, ten 16X internal CD-ROM drives, two 9.1 GB hard drives, plus one 2.1 GB hard drive
Software: *Workstation:* Microsoft Windows 95, Microsoft Internet Explorer, Menu Builder, Fortres and Ikiosk security programs
Server: Microsoft Windows NT 4.0
Programs: Contemporary Authors, Current Biography, Reader's Guide, InfoTrac Search Bank, FirstSearch core and specialized databases, SIRS Researcher, Masterplots, Exegy, SIRS Government Reporter CD-ROM, Grolier Multimedia Encyclopedia, Encyclopedia Americana, Diskport Executive CD-ROM
Description: The goal of this project was to provide beginning-reading-age youth to 14-year-olds access to electronic reference sources. Participants had access to a wide variety of online and CD-ROM reference sources provided by a network to a subset of resources on the Adult Services reference server. The library staff believes that youth need access to quality reference sources mediated by staff who can teach while guiding youth through the process.

Individuals can sign up for two nonconsecutive half-hour sessions per day. If no one is signed up for the consecutive session, the individual may take that session. The library provides ten free pages of paper per day. Additional paper may be purchased at 10¢ a sheet.

Youth need a lot of individual attention to guide them through their searching. Having staff available to assist them is critical to the youths' success and satisfaction. Since the Internet is the most popular option on these machines, access to periodical indexes and other core tools is compromised during busy times. Two options are being explored to solve this: (1) provide two more machines, one with everything but Internet, or (2) put all resources but the Internet as selections on the OPAC.

Project length: Ongoing

Cost: Some hardware (server, network lines) and all software is shared by various library divisions. The 1998 cost for CD-ROM and online reference sources is $58,600. Cost for Youth Services workstations is $1,500 each. Funding came from a Library Budget and Major Urban Resource Libraries Grant from the State of Illinois.

Circulation Systems and Online Catalogs

A variety of microcomputer circulation and online catalog systems used in special, academic, school, and public libraries are represented in this chapter. These systems include standard off-the-shelf circulation systems, circulation systems created from scratch using scripts, and off-the-shelf database systems. The Blough-Weis Library at Susquehanna University uses Microsoft Access to circulate AV hardware, software, and accessories to faculty to support course work. The Sulzer Regional Library of the Chicago Public Library created its own Macintosh-based videotape circulation system from scratch using FoxPro. It circulates a 15,000-videotape collection to bring in more than $120,000 in rentals each year.

There are many fine microcomputer software packages for making catalog cards and for creating an online public catalog at affordable prices. Many libraries, especially school and special libraries, have used such packages to make their materials more accessible.

Name:	**Circulation and Cataloging in a University Library**
Library:	Robert Wood Johnson Medical School, University of Medicine and Dentistry of New Jersey
Contact:	Zana Etter, director
Address:	Robert Wood Johnson Medical School, University of Medicine and Dentistry of New Jersey, Piscataway, NJ 08854
Phone:	(732) 235-4671; Fax: (732) 235-4117
E-mail:	etter@rwja.umdnj.edu
Hardware:	486 Compaq Prolinea 450
Software:	EOS International Managers Series version 7.1, WordPerfect, Microsoft Word for Windows
Description:	The introduction of the circulation module in 1989 provided an excellent control mechanism for tracking borrowers and items and allowed statistical reports to be created. In 1994, the catalog

module was added. Most items are still processed using this DOS-based system. A need to move to an integrated Windows environment is anticipated shortly. When new computers are installed, it is planned to migrate to the EOS International GLAS product, which will enable users to use an OPAC that is currently not available. Also purchased was EOS International's Data-bridge module, which will eventually allow records to be captured and imported into the catalog module, thus streamlining the cataloging procedure. WordPerfect or Word for Windows is used when creating lists or doing word processing for library-related tasks.

Project length:	Since 1989 for circulation, since 1994 for cataloging
Cost:	One-time request from Dean's office; software and a support contract paid for through operating budget of approximately $19,000 per year

Name:	**Circulation System in a Special Library**
Library:	Gerber Hart Library and Archive
Contact:	Russell Kracke
Address:	1127 W. Granville, Chicago, IL 60660
Phone:	(773) 883-3003
Web site:	http://www.gerberhart.org
Hardware:	Packard Bell Pentium, Hewlett Packard Laser-4P printer and DeskJet 600c printer
Software:	Microsoft Office 4.2, WordPerfect 6.0, QuickBooks, Columbia Library System
Description:	This library and archive serves the gay, lesbian, bisexual, and transgendered community. It uses Microsoft Office 4.2 to circulate its collection of approximately 8,000 books, 5,000 serials, and a variety of information in other formats. The two PCs and other hardware are stand-alone; the library does not yet have a LAN. One PC keeps track of materials patrons check out and the due date. The other PC is used for library budgeting. QuickBooks creates monthly and annual reports of income and expenditures, accounts payable, accounts receivable, and invoices. The core of the library's setup is the Columbia Library System, a DOS-based online catalog system that provides records of all library materials. It also serves as an online public access catalog.
Project length:	Ongoing
Cost:	All funds were made available through grants, memberships, donations, and a fund-raiser; exact project cost is unknown

Circulation Systems and Online Catalogs 27

Name: **Media-Booking Database**
Library: Blough-Weis Library, Susquehanna University
Contact: Rebecca A. Wilson
Address: 514 University Ave., Selinsgrove, PA 17870-1050
E-mail: wilson@roo.susqu.edu
Hardware: IBM Pentium PC
Software: Microsoft Access
Description: The Blough-Weis Library Media Center schedules AV hardware and accessories, software, and facilities for use in course work. As the collections and number of reservations have increased, record keeping graduated from a calendar, to a form, to a database maintained with Microsoft Access. AV equipment and video titles are on separate tables, classrooms as well as AV facilities are on another, and an additional table is for reservations.

The faculty requests a facility and/or a title for a certain date and time, and Media Center staff check to be sure there are no reservation conflicts. If there are none, the data is entered into the database. If a prior reservation has been made for that date/time, an alternative is found and entered into the database.

A table with reservations for multimedia equipment is kept separately to see at a glance when the multimedia equipment (notebooks, LCD projectors, and accessories) is available. Queries will list everything scheduled for a date or for a faculty member and to list the scheduled video titles by date or in alphabetical order. Reports can be generated for the day's activities and for each faculty member's reservation. The tables, queries, and reports are pulled together under a macro.
Project length: 1997–present
Cost: None; project uses existing hardware and software

Name: **Online Catalog in a Corporate Library**
Library: Santee Cooper Corporate Library
Contact: Suzanne Krebsbach
Address: One Riverwood Dr., Moncks Corner, SC 29461
Phone: (843) 761-4072
E-mail: SMKREBSB@sontp.santeecooper.com
Hardware: Dell 486 PC
Software: EOS International GLAS Series
Description: The Santee Cooper Corporate Library is a one-person library that contracts with OCLC to provide cataloging for its 20,000-volume collection. GOPAC (a Windows-based Graphical Online Public

Access Catalog) is mounted on the corporate Intranet. As data is received from OCLC, it is used to update the cataloging module (and thus the GOPAC module). The goal was to find a way to provide online access to the library's resources for the 1,600 users scattered across South Carolina. By August 1998, approximately 50 percent of the goal had been reached. The International GLAS Series is a Windows-based library automation package with modules for circulation, cataloging, serials, online public access catalogs, inventory, and other functions.

Project length: 1997–1999
Cost: Annual budget

Name: **Our Lady of Mount Carmel Parish Online Catalog**
Library: Our Lady of Mount Carmel Parish, Carmel Prayer Center Library
Contacts: Sr. Benedicta; Virginia R. Reed
Address: Sr. Benedicta (or Virginia Reed), Our Lady of Mount Carmel Parish, Carmel Center Library, 708 W. Belmont Ave., Chicago, IL 60657
Phone: (773) 477-6836
Hardware: Gateway 2000 PC, 386DX/33 MHz
Software: Microsoft Windows 3.1, Microsoft Works File Manager
Description: Our Lady of Mount Carmel Parish has approximately 2,800 members. The collection consists of approximately 2,000 books and 300 audiotapes of religious or spiritual content. The books are shelved by broad subject classifications, and the tapes are shelved by number.

The computer listing contains author, title, date of publication, classification (or location number for tapes), subject 1 (for personal names) and subject 2 (for subjects), and an entry date. This listing makes it possible to produce leaflets on various subjects that are used by prayer and study groups. Leaflets can be prepared by author or subject, as biographies, or in conjunction with the parish lecture series.

The complete book collection has not yet been added to the computer file, and a partial listing without subjects has been initiated to facilitate access. By using the "find" command, users can locate materials that have a subject word in the title. The audiotapes are all on the computer files, and a listing by subject is available.

Project length: Ongoing

Name:	**Sulzer Videotape Management System and Integrated Ordering System**
Library:	Sulzer Regional Library, Chicago Public Library
Contact:	Marvin Garber
Address:	4455 N. Lincoln Ave., Chicago, IL 60625
Phone:	(312) 744-7616
E-mail:	MarvinG1@aol.com
Hardware:	Macintosh SE/30m Uucx, 2 Color Classic printers, 2 Apple Laser printers, Canon Bubble-Jet printer, 4 laser scanners or wand bar-code readers
Software:	FoxPro multiuser, custom programs written in the Foxbase language similar to dBase language, AppleShare network
Description:	The Chicago Public Library serves the millions of residents of the City of Chicago and provides reciprocal borrowing and services to surrounding communities and to the State of Illinois. The Sulzer Regional Library houses some 15,000 videotapes that bring in approximately $120,000 per year in revenue. A complete in-house circulation system was created (programmed) from scratch to handle the more than 4,300 video rentals per week. This project is an excellent example of how librarians use existing equipment to create specialized software for a particular function.

It is suggested that the person who writes the programs should use the system to gain a fuller understanding of user needs. System design can then be easily modified as needs change.

Prior to the installation of this system, videotapes were not cataloged and were checked out manually. The new system provides for full circulation functions, including fee calculation, audit, patron records, fine calculation, holds, and report generation. It also has an online ordering component and can print charge transaction notices. Informal cataloging is done by local staff and entered into the system.

Reports include delinquent notices; an overdue items list; a daily report of circulation and fees; and formatted lists of videos by title, subject keyword, cast name, director name, series, language, and author of original work. |
| Project length: | 1991–present |
| Cost: | $15,000 (estimate) |

Computer Centers and Labs

Running a computer center or lab is a full-time job. Many labs involve a local area network (LAN), while others are a hodgepodge of stand-alone machines. A LAN affords the sharing of printers, CD-ROMs, and other peripherals as well as convenient access to the Internet.

Some of the problems and matters to consider when operating a lab (or any public access facility) include how to charge users who print documents, locate knowledgeable lab assistants, make appointments, train the public in various aspects of computer literacy, and basic use of the Internet. The Internet creates an entire set of problems that range from pornography to being swamped by users who monopolize all available computers to access chat rooms and other cyberspace entertainments.

Another significant problem that often arises for labs is failing to take adequate steps to repair or replace aging or broken equipment. One computer center had a room full of computers that had been purchased through a special grant program. As the equipment aged and needed repair, the library administration declined to fix anything. After about three years, nothing worked, and the lab is now unused.

Solutions to these problems can include installation of filtering systems such as Cyber Patrol to protect children from X-rated materials, hiring high school and college students as lab assistants, having a computer technician on call when needed, offering special classes, developing flyers and handouts to train the public, and using key-card systems for vending laser printers. (Some libraries charge for printing; some do not.)

Name:	**Law Library's Computer Labs**
Library:	Gonzaga University Library
Address:	East 502 Boone Ave., Spokane, WA 99258
E-mail:	http://www.law.gonzaga.edu/library
Hardware:	25 IBM compatible PCs with 100 MHz Pentium processors, 256 K cache, 16 MB RAM on Trident chipset video cards, low radiation 14″ super VGA monitors; Microsoft mice; scanner

Software:	Computer Assisted Legal Instruction (CALI), career services databases, FileMaker Pro, EagleNet Resources, IMAP Mail Client, LEXIS/NEXIS databases, Microsoft Excel, Microsoft Word, Netscape Navigator, Norton Utilities, Microsoft PowerPoint, QUEST, UVIEW, WESTLAW databases, Congressional Masterfile 1 and 2, Hein's United Nations Treaty Index, Health Care Financing Administration database, LegalTrac index, Massachusetts Administrative Law Library, NELLICO Union Catalog, Nuremberg Trial Transcripts
Description:	The Law Library's lab has Macintosh computers and IBM PCs available for staff, faculty, and law school students. It is open concurrently with library hours and is staffed by student assistants. Law students are provided with passwords to the computer lab. The password can also be used to use Internet e-mail. Disk space is provided on the GULAW2 network server for saving files.

Lab users have access to a great deal of law-related information. Computer Assisted Legal Instruction (CALI) provides instruction in accounting, administrative law, civil procedure, commercial transactions, contracts, corporate law, criminal law, employment discrimination, environmental law, evidence, federal courts, insurance law, labor law, legal research and writing, professional responsibility, property law, sales, securities regulation, taxation, torts, wills, and trusts.

LEXIS and WESTLAW are located in rooms on Level 1 of the library on 10 workstations. The databases contain legal materials on legislation, court decisions, administrative regulations and decisions, and law review articles. Reference staff also offer periodic training sessions for basic and advanced skills on these databases. First-year students are given training on either LEXIS or WESTLAW.

CD-ROM databases are networked. They include Congressional Masterfile 1 & 2 (indexes and abstracts to United States congressional publications), Health Care Financing Administration (laws, regulations, and manuals of the HCFA), Hein's United Nations Treaty Index, LegalTrac (index to legal periodicals and newspapers), Massachusetts Administrative Law Library (Code of Massachusetts Regulations and selected Massachusetts administrative agency decisions), NELLICO Union Catalog (catalog of materials held by member libraries of the New England Law Library Consortium), and Nuremberg Trial Transcripts (full text of the trials before the International Military Tribunal set in Nuremberg).

Project length:	1995–present in its current configuration; additional upgrades planned

Name:	**Library of the Health Sciences Twenty-Four-Hour Microcomputer Lab**
Library:	College of Medicine at Rockford, University of Illinois
Address:	1601 Parkview Ave., Rockford, IL 61107
Phone:	(815) 395-5650
Hardware:	*Library lab:* computers: Macintosh IIcx, Classic, Classic II, IIci, Centris 650, 2 IBM PC XTs (used as network terminals), 1 Dell 433s/L, Interserve Computer Group ICG; printers: Personal LaserWriter NT, Hewlett Packard LaserJet series II, Epson FX100; laser disk player
	Twenty-four-hour lab: 3 Dell 433/L, 1 Epson Equity IIe, 3 Macintosh Centris 650, 1 Apple Personal LaserWriter Pro 630
Software:	Word processing, studyware, and course-related programs
Description:	The Library of the Health Sciences, University of Illinois, maintains two on-site computer labs. One is open during regular library hours. The other is available twenty-four hours per day. The twenty-four-hour lab is controlled by a key-card system. The labs provide microcomputer and Internet services to staff, faculty, and students of the College of Medicine. In addition to word processing and educational programs for course-related subjects, access is also provided to the Academic Data Network that connects to mainframe and UNIX computers in Chicago. Users may also search the National Library of Medicine databases (for example, MEDLINE) and can send and receive e-mail.
	The library lab computers can be reserved, and reservations are held for 15 minutes, after which they are given to someone else. The twenty-four-hour lab can be reserved by faculty for a class. Unreserved computers can also be used by walk-ins on a first-come, first-serve basis to anyone with a key card. Both the library lab and the twenty-four-hour lab provide guides and tutorials for programs. In the twenty-four-hour lab, limited help is available from library staff Monday through Friday, 8 A.M. to 4:30 P.M. All equipment in the library lab is turned off five minutes prior to the library closing.
Reference:	www.uic.edu/depts/mrad/campus/library/libmiclb.html
Project length:	Ongoing

Name:	**Library Open-Access Computer Lab**
Library:	JFK Library, California State University, Los Angeles, California, Academic Technology Support
Address:	5151 State University Dr., Los Angeles, CA 90032-8300
Phone:	(323) 343-3950

Hardware:	PCs and Macs with printers connected to a LAN
Software:	Windows 98/NT, Microsoft Word, Excel, PowerPoint, Access, Outlook, Internet Explorer; FileMaker Pro; Netscape Navigator
Description:	The JFK Library computer lab requires a student I.D. for access. To use the laser printers in the lab requires use of the VendaCoder Dispenser. Users first purchase a $1 VendCard, then add value of $1 to $99 in even-dollar amounts to it. When users want to print, they insert their card and the appropriate charge is deducted from it. Although this is handy and avoids staff involvement, the original outlay is expensive and is a good idea only for libraries with a high volume of printing that can provide a return on the investment. An explanation of the use and retrieval of output from laser printers at the Cal State L.A. Academic Technology Support is at http://www.we.calstatela.edu/ats/isis/library/prtretr.htm. Another Web page provides complete instructions for using the VendaCoder at http://www.we.calstatela.edu/ats/isis/library/venda.htm.

A number of student training programs are available that include an introduction to the campus network, introduction to the Internet, using the modem pool, Scholar's Mail, Microsoft Excel 5 for Windows, Microsoft Word 6 for Windows, Microsoft PowerPoint 4 for Windows, and Microsoft Access 2.0 for Windows. These are free computer workshops that change from semester to semester. The Introduction to the Campus Network is for beginners and provides an introduction to the Campus Network, including the resources available through the Scholar's Work Environment, an academic tool available in the labs and electronic classrooms. The workshop provides the groundwork for available resources and an introduction to access research tools such as JFK Library OPAC, LEXIS-NEXIS, and Silver-Platter databases. Students receive personal storage space on the network. They learn to use Telnet, FTP, and e-mail. Other highlights include an introduction to student accounts, account information, and more.

Reference:	http://www.calstatela.edu/ats/labs/labrules/index.htm
Project length:	Ongoing

Name:	**Little Village Learning and Literacy Center**
Library:	John Toman Branch Library, Chicago Public Library
Contact:	Jim Smith, branch librarian
Address:	4005 W. 27th St., Chicago, IL 60623
Phone:	(312) 747-8115; Fax: (312) 747-8116

Hardware: IBM server, 5 IBM PC II 386, 2 printers
Software: Centex WICAT, various educational programs for nonnetworked general adult public access
Description: The dual purpose of this computerized learning center was to provide training for adult literacy and for general public access such as word processing, etc. It was intended for use by all age groups for individualized instruction in a variety of subject areas; for use with an English as a Second Language (ESL) class and existing network of Chicago City College classes in ESL; for GED (General Education Development) instruction and ABE (Adult Basic Education) classes, and for use by the existing network of community grassroots educational systems. The learning center at the library supported and supplemented alternative and continuing educational programs and initiatives throughout the community, and gave teachers and tutors (especially volunteer teachers and tutors) and students a major tool and resource for the conduct of alternative education.

To some extent, the project was also an experiment. While staff at Toman had considerable experience with literacy and alternative educational programming, it was still an open question as to how effective the library could be in the general literacy initiative. It was not entirely clear how far the library, especially a branch library, should commit to direct involvement in the process of public education. In the end, the program proved overly ambitious but much was learned.

To a great extent, success of this project depended on the network of ESL, GED, literacy, and ABE classes that existed when the project was planned. Unfortunately, as the project moved into the implementation phase, Chicago City Colleges began to seriously downsize its network of classes, and funding was cut or reduced to many other agencies and organizations that were supporting literacy or other alternative educational programs. This seriously reduced the Center's potential. The library was probably never in a position to become a primary literacy provider (as now defined), but without an efficient network of classes, students, teachers, and tutors to use and support the Learning Center, it left the library in a position of having to recruit students and provide primary instruction. The equipment has remained available for public use after the project concluded.

Project length: 1992–1993
Cost: $135,000 through an LSCA Title I grant

Name:	**Mobile Public Online Computer Services (The MOBILE Project)**
Libraries:	Netherlands Centre for Libraries and Literature (NBLC); Carpenter Davies Associates; Scottish Borders Council Library Service; CBS Friesland; and the public library in Veria, Western Macedonia, Greece
Contact:	Julie Carpenter, senior partner, Carpenter Davies Associates
Address:	33 Arnold Rd., Oxford OX1 4BH, UK
E-mail:	j.carpenter@efc.co.uk
Hardware:	computers and related equipment
Software:	CD-ROM databases, local information sources, computer application programs, library catalog
Description:	The MOBILE project's central goal is to provide information electronically through vehicles similar in nature to traditional bookmobiles. Objectives include making services available to target groups that are not currently served through traditional locations and libraries.

The project was planned in three stages. The first stage was the evaluation of potential user groups and information needs not met in other ways. The second stage was the running of trials of vehicles and services for one year among the user groups. The third stage was an analysis of the field trials.

It is interesting to note the services and information sources available through this electronic bookmobile include an online and many CD-ROM databases. It also includes the areas of tourism, financial market data, and programs, etc., of the European Union. Such community services as "regional statutory and voluntary sector organizations" and local, regional, and Scottish history (provided by a phone/fax that linked the van to a reference library headquarters) were also considered important enough to include. The library catalog on hard disk was made available for reference use and for reserving library materials. Onboard fax and photocopying services were also provided.

To ascertain potential users and their needs, 545 extensive questionnaires were completed. It was found that 51 percent of users were retired, 21 percent sought information from another country (for example, for travel), and 15 percent sought welfare or social assistance.

According to the MOBILE project final report, the value of the work carried out included exposing inequalities inherent in the European, market-driven telecommunications infrastructure in terms of coverage and quality, speed of development, and costs. The report highlighted the difficulties of navigating effectively through many publicly accessible but unorganized networked information sources under cost and time pressures. The project demonstrated decisively the effectiveness and high potential of CD-ROM and multimedia technology in a mobile library environment. It drew attention to the need for greater flexibility in time tabling and staffing mobile library service points and demonstrated the paucity of quality electronic and networked information in European languages other than English.

The report includes a list of what could or should be done differently in the future, including having fewer partners. "It was overambitious, given the limited resources at the disposal of the Partners, to attempt to trial MOBILE services in three library organizations: the project would have been more effective and manageable if only one Northern European library had participated. The identification of definable groups of potential users (e.g., in education, in local government, or business) who were not already users of the mobile library services . . . might have produced indications of clear user demands . . . and clear targets for the project." The report concludes that "the project would have benefitted from a preliminary 'feasibility' phase resulting in a tighter focus for the 'demonstration' phase."

Reference:	Sarah Ormes and Lorcan Dempsey, eds., *The Internet, Networking and the Public Library* (London, Eng.: Library Association Publishing, 1997).
Project length:	May 1996–present
Cost:	£470,000; costs shared among the five project partners and the European Commission

Name:	**Portage-Cragin Branch Library Computer Center Building Program**
Library:	Portage-Cragin Branch, Chicago Public Library
Contact:	Kevin Latham
Address:	5108 W. Belmont Ave., Chicago, IL 60641
Phone:	(312) 744-2820
E-mail:	klatham@hotmail.com
Hardware:	2 Apple IIgs computers with Apple ImageWriter II printers, 3 IBM PS/2 computers with 2 Panasonic KX-P1191 dot matrix printers, 1 Macintosh SE and 1 Macintosh IIsi computers each with a Hewlett Packard LaserWriter II printer, 4 Compaq Pentium DeskPro computers with 3 Hewlett Packard LaserJet printers and 1 Lexmark Optra R+ printer
Software:	More than 50 Apple II educational titles for juveniles; 30 DOS-

based educational titles for juveniles; 50 popular titles for Macintosh including word processing, spreadsheet, graphics, and database packages; more than 50 DOS, Windows, and Windows 95-based programs for adults including word processing, spreadsheet, graphics, and database packages; tutorials

Description: The goal of the project was to create a public access computer center, a separate addition to the Portage-Cragin Branch Library, to give Chicago-area residents free access to a variety of computers, equipment, and software and to computer book and magazine collections. The center is staffed with a full-time librarian who offers assistance and instruction.

Students use the center to do homework and produce school reports. Adults use it to create résumés, letters, and papers. Users of all ages and computer abilities come to the center to learn more about computers and software. The computer center currently offers free introductory classes on the Internet. The computer center is open to the public Monday through Thursday from 1 P.M. to 7 P.M. and on Saturdays from 10 A.M. to 4 P.M.

Anyone planning a computer center should do some research on its location, equipment, software, and staffing. The most helpful thing for anyone planning a center would be to visit existing computer centers. A crucial factor to the success of the center in a library environment is its location and design. The center should be a separate or isolated area so that neither library patrons nor computer center patrons are disturbed. In designing a center, sufficient space and ventilation should be provided for both patrons and computers.

Computer center staff members should have as their main or only duty working in the center. This additional staff needed for the computer center should be factored into the yearly library budget.

A carefully thought-out policy for patron computer use will minimize problems. It should be completed prior to the opening of a center. Allow time for the library administration to approve the policy.

It is essential to maintain open communication between library and computer center staff. The library will need to understand the basics of the computer center operations and policy. It is also helpful to train both the computer center and library staff in computer use.

Project length: 1987–present
Cost: $500,000, of which $105,000 was for furniture, software, and equipment; funded through a Build Illinois LSCA grant

Name:	**Public Computer Labs**
Library:	King County Library System
Contact:	Nancy Smith
Address:	300 Eighth Ave. N., Seattle, WA 98109
Phone:	(206) 296-5291
E-mail:	nancsmit@kcls.org
Hardware:	20 PC workstations; 2 servers, 1 network printer
Software:	Microsoft PowerPoint, Microsoft Publisher, Microsoft Excel, Microsoft Access, and several programs for children and a host of minor programs that are regularly updated and expanded
Description:	The purpose of the computer labs is to help the public develop basic computer skills and perform useful computer work. Using the available software, patrons may create letters and other personal documents, improve their typing with a typing tutorial, make computer-generated presentations for display, edit and style newsletters, manipulate spreadsheets, create databases, and write résumés with a special stand-alone résumé program. Programs specially created for children are also available, and graphical access to the Internet is provided. Both videotape and software tutorials, manuals, and classes are available for assistance. The use of the lab and its materials is free, but computer use requires an appointment. Free training sessions in the form of classes are provided on a regular basis. Students must register in advance.

The labs must maintain security to prevent hacking on the PCs. Local staff time (other than PC trainers) is required for lab-related duties—approximately 30 hours per week. Support by technicians is an additional cost factor. |
Reference:	http://www.kcls.org/kcls/computerlabs.html
Project length:	December 1997–present
Cost:	Start-up: $110,000 for equipment and supplies; $24,000 for PC trainer's salary; $20,000 for operating budget

Name:	**U.S. Navy Library Media Resource Center**
Library:	NSA Library, Naples, Italy
Contact:	Robert Adamshick
Address:	NSA Library, PSC 817, Box 09, FPO, AE 09622-0922
Hardware:	6 Nexas computers, Hewlett Packard ScanJet, Hewlett Packard LaserJet 4000 printer
Software:	Microsoft Windows 95

Description:	The Library Media Resource Center is at a U.S. Naval base library in Naples, Italy. It attempts to fulfill the naval personnel's many microcomputer needs. The center has four computers for Internet access. In addition, the computers are also used for making schedules, book ordering, and signage for various base operations. A CD-ROM tower contains seven drives for various popular programs. The new computers have been a huge success with usage of the library soaring since they were installed.
Project length:	April 1998–present
Cost:	Centrally funded by U.S. Navy for Mediterranean region

Desktop Publishing and Graphics

Library staff use microcomputer software to publish and create graphics for newsletters (including print and online), banners, signs, invitations, slide shows, and much more. A good desktop publishing program, such as Microsoft Publisher, allows users to mix graphics and text on the same page, create multicolumn newsletters, and do a variety of other tasks. One of the most popular packages for many years is Print Shop. Though not a full desktop publisher, it comes with a variety of clip art and boilerplate styles for basic products. It also has a variety of add-on modules available. Anyone can use it to create sophisticated banners, invitations, posters, and other materials in minutes. In addition to these packages specifically geared to creating graphic products, packages such as WordPerfect can be used for the same thing, although the startup time may be longer. WordPerfect can be used to create a sophisticated newsletter or booklet complete with graphics. It comes with a variety of newsletter and other templates.

The elements of desktop publishing include content planning, font selection, graphics placement, and column selection.

Name:	**Electronic Products Showcase: A Slide Show**
Library:	University of Saskatchewan Libraries
Contact:	Darlene Fichter
Address:	215–116 Research Dr., Saskatoon, SK Canada S7N 3R3
Phone:	(306) 966-7209
E-mail:	Darlene.Fichter@usask.ca
Hardware:	Pentium PC
Software:	PolyView, PolyView Screensaver, Microsoft PowerPoint, Paintshop Pro
Description:	The University of Saskatchewan Libraries has created a number of electronic collections and courses. To facilitate demonstrating these projects at a library conference, a slide show in the form of a screen saver was created and shown on a PC. Initially, 20

screen snapshots from electronic products were captured using Paintshop Pro. Headings and separator pages were easily and quickly created in PowerPoint and saved as screen snapshots. At this point, using the PolyView Screensaver programs, the various files were selected for the show.

Using an incremental numbering scheme for the slides that matches the sequence of the show helps save time. The program allows the timing for the slide rotation to be set, sounds added, and special effects included. Once the show is complete, it is saved. PolyView Screensaver is set up as the default screen saver by right clicking the mouse button on the desktop background, choosing Properties, and choosing "PolyView Screensaver" or "Pvsaver" from the list of screen savers presented. The PolyView Screensaver module can only be used by registered users.

References:	PolyView: http://www.polyview.com
	PolyView Slide Show specification window: http://www.polyview.com/shots.html#SSSELECT
Project length:	May 6–9, 1998
Cost:	$25 fixed costs, two days' development time

Name:	**Library News & Notes: An Electronic Newsletter for Faculty**
Library:	The Thomas M. Cooley Law School Library
Contact:	Aletha L. Honsowitz, head of educational services
Address:	217 S. Capital Ave., P.O. Box 13038, Lansing, MI 48901
Phone:	(517) 371-5140 x611
E-mail:	honsowia@cooley.edu
Hardware:	Pentium PC
Software:	WordPerfect 6.1, 7.0, and 8.0; Netscape Navigator or Internet Explorer; Netscape Communicator 4.0
Description:	The goal of this project was to enhance and promote electronic communication with the faculty by regularly sending information about library services, products, and technology to all Thomas Cooley faculty via the medium of e-mail. To further promote technology, the Library News & Notes moved to the Thomas M. Cooley Web site in July 1998. The library's faculty-liaison program is a great communication tool. The newsletter features announcements, interesting Web sites, recent library acquisitions, faculty cited (in law review articles, etc.), and library staff out this week. Links are provided to sites so that a reader may quickly link to and bookmark the site. A cumulative index to the Library News & Notes with links is issued and verified each term and loaded on the Web. Newsletters are kept on

the Web during the term in which they first appear, then deleted. Archival copies of all issues are available in the Cooley Library.

Planning is essential, and includes deciding on the type of information to convey, determining reader interests, developing a way to reach a large faculty with varied interests, and providing something for everyone. Another consideration is technology. Sending the newsletter via e-mail creates many difficulties, including compatibility of formats for different e-mail systems. When the newsletter moved to the Web, these problems were resolved.

Staff involvement depends on a variety of factors. Originally the newsletter took 8 to 16 hours per week to produce. Preparing to put the newsletter on the Web required that staff learn basic HTML and Communicator 4.0. It now takes 4 to 6 hours per week to locate information, write, edit, and send the newsletter to the Webmaster. A suggestion is to assign sections of the newsletter to different staff members and have them submit the information on disk. Although time-consuming to produce, the newsletter is an excellent communication tool that compels the faculty to use technology.

Reference: http://www.cooley.edu
Project length: March 1997–present

Name: **Plainedge Public Library Program Newsletter**
Library: Plainedge Public Library
Contact: Joseph Eisner
Address: 1060 Hicksville Rd., Massapequa, NY 11758
Phone: (516) 735-4133
E-mail: PELSUPER@NASSAU.NLS.LIB.NY.US
Hardware: IBM PC compatible, Pentium 100, 16 MB RAM
Software: Adobe PageMaker 6.5
Description: Plainedge Public Library staff have been producing a newsletter in one form or another for the past 25 years. Their current newsletter is produced almost entirely by computer six times each year using PageMaker 6.5. The newsletter contains program and services information, one- or two-page consumer bulletins, and a readers' messages section.

In addition to the newsletter, the library produces or reproduces seven different publications. *News for the ConsUmer* is produced every three weeks. It includes four to six pages of informative articles on health, energy, money management, etc. Every two years it includes a list, by category, of available consumer bulletins, issues of *News for the ConsUmer,* and other agency publications. The information for this publication is made available from public domain sources such as Cooperative Extension Service of New York State, U.S. Food and Drug Administration, U.S. Department of Agriculture, state and Nassau County agencies, and others. Permission is also occasionally obtained to reproduce informative articles from publications such as *Family Circle, Woman's Day,* and the *New York Times.* Often, royalty fees are waived for the library on the condition that proper credit is given.

Community Courier is a quarterly, six- to eight-page publication designed to give area residents topical news and information they will not see in a single source elsewhere. Information includes news releases from the county executive, town supervisor, county office of consumer affairs, and local assembly members and senator. Special articles are occasionally commissioned about Plainedge events and needs. A community calendar lists meetings and events by Plainedge groups. A News of Your Neighbors section highlights area anniversaries, graduations, promotions, and similar events. Camera-ready copy is sent to the printers for reproduction.

Another publication, *Discovery*, is mailed quarterly to 1,000 citizens in the service area. This two-sided self-mailer sometimes includes special "alerts" for seniors that advise them of special opportunities such as free Pap smears, inoculations, etc.

SUNBURST/EXPAND is published six times each year. It is mailed to some 200 parents of children in the Plainedge School District's gifted program at the elementary and junior high school levels.

Pierre the Pelican is geared to prenatal/postnatal service. It is mailed first class to 123 parents and produced by the National Mental Health Association.

PERS (Plainedge Employment Referral Service) was published twice-yearly and mailed to 2,800 local area employers. It has been changed to a postcard reminder that advises employers of listings available that can be sent upon request.

Reference:	Joseph Eisner, "Disseminating Library-Produced Information by Direct Mail," *RQ* 32 (winter 1994): 150.
Project length:	Ongoing
Cost:	Printing costs $865 per issue; mailing costs $543 per issue nonprofit bulk rate; labor costs $2,750 (composition and data entry), $183 (addressing) for six issues; total $11,396 per year from library operating budget

Name:	**Production of *Library Links:* A Quarterly Newsletter**
Library:	Calumet City Public Library
Contact:	Vickie L. Novak, library director
Address:	660 Manistee Ave., Calumet City, IL 60409
Phone:	(708) 862-6220 x244
E-mail:	novakv@sls.lib.il.us
Hardware:	Macintosh Centris 610, Apple LaserWriter Pro, Hewlett Packard ScanJet Plus Scanner
Software:	Ready, Set, Go! 6.0
Description:	The Calumet City Public Library wanted a professional, eye-catching newsletter at a reasonable price. To eliminate expensive setup charges, etc., it needed to be totally "camera-ready" before it went to the printer. Due to its reputation for ease of operation, particularly in the area of desktop publishing, a Macintosh was chosen. The original issues were produced on a Mac II. The Calumet City Library was one of the first public libraries in the country to have this "high-powered" computer available ten years ago. Since that time, equipment and software have been upgraded several times. The library director edits and produces the newsletter, having gathered information from all department heads. The library has received numerous compliments on the newsletter's layout and straightforward design. In fact, it has been featured at the ALA Annual Swap 'N' Shop. The newsletter is called *Library Links*.
Project length:	June 1988–present
Cost:	$9,000, including postage and printing, from a per-capita grant

Indexing

Many libraries create indexes. Often these are of the local newspaper for the local history collection. Some libraries create special indexes for collections of books, periodicals, obituaries, etc. Indexing may be carried out using a database program such as dBase or Visual FoxPro or a word processing program such as WordPerfect. Most local history indexes consist of just a few fields, and the resulting product may be used as a printout for public use.

Among the projects in this section is that of the Eisenhower Public Library, which used Microsoft Word to make a simple database of song titles for songs contained in books owned by the library. It also created a list of obituaries in local papers. The Mishawaka-Penn Public Library created an index of auto repair manuals owned by the library.

Name:	**Christian County Indexes**
Library:	Christian County Library
Contact:	Mabel G. Phillips
Address:	1005 N. 4th Ave., Ozark, MO 65721
Phone:	(417) 581-2432
E-mail:	ruf002@mail.connect.more.net
Hardware:	8088 Tandy; donated $5\frac{1}{4}''$ diskettes; 286, 386, 486, and Pentium PCs
Software:	Microsoft Works
Description:	The library began the creation of electronic databases to provide a one-stop index by place and time of official and/or published records of people who have lived in Christian County, Missouri. All "people" databases begin with the same fields: birth surname, given name, latest surname, life span, son/daughter, and parents. These databases include census, marriage, deeds, land tax, personal property tax, cemetery, funeral home, organizational records, and published sources indexes. Each has fields

appropriate to that database such as part, township, range, and section on land taxes; book and page, spouse, date, residence of groom and bride, and official on marriages; and year, state, county, subdivision, and household for census records. Databases are then cross-matched to identify records believed almost certainly to belong to the same individual. Researchers could then look at these references to draw their own conclusions.

A warning to those creating such a project is to be aware of the volume of work involved. This project for a small county is estimated to be about 16,000 hours. Anyone attempting this sort of project should guard also against the danger of loss or corruption of data. A group of individual workers could do it best. Perhaps one could cover marriages, deaths, organizations, events, and locations; another tax records, censuses, etc. All would need to be familiar enough with the history to recognize names in difficult handwriting, to be extremely careful about completeness and accuracy, and to work together on format and database development.

The library has done all the work outside library hours. The library bought some local records microfilm, made some trips to the state archives to have some loaned records microfilmed, and photocopied some other loaned materials to allow time to input the data while returning the records quickly. The funding includes two LSCA grants, one to hire someone for two weeks to enter some recent information gathered from businesses and organizations and a second to provide a computer and printer to give direct public access to the database. Although the cost is not known, a library friend in New Mexico devoted a Web site to host some of the smaller databases. Others have photocopied or microfilmed official organizational or company (for example, funeral home) records at their expense for inclusion. Individual files will be switched to Microsoft Access as they reach the maximum record threshold of 32,000.

Reference: Examples of some of the smaller databases are at http://home.sprynet.com/sprynet/jenwbber/ccm.htm
Project length: 1989–present
Cost: See discussion; in 1997, an LSCA grant of $3,050 for a computer and printer

Name: **Electronic Index of Auto-Repair Manuals**
Library: Mishawaka-Penn Public Library
Contact: Dennis C. Tucker

Indexing   47

Address:	Dennis C. Tucker, 6202 Morenci Tr., Indianapolis, IN 46268
Phone:	(317) 298-6570
E-mail:	Dennis@palni.edu
Hardware:	IBM PC compatible
Software:	PC-File
Description:	To participate in cooperative collection development with other area libraries, the library needed to convert the contents of its automobile repair manuals to an electronic index. Patrons needing such manuals came to the Mishawaka-Penn Public Library and often would not find the work on the shelf. Then they would turn to the reference desk for assistance. Realizing that finding the proper information would be much easier if reference staff could easily determine which books contained information on particular models, it was decided to create an electronic index. Using the electronic database program PC-File, fields were created for automobile make (for example, Chevrolet), model (Bel Air), and year as well as the title and call number of the book containing the information. A student staff member reviewed the table of contents of each car repair manual in the collection for this information and entered it into the database. The ability to meet patrons' needs made it worthwhile. The project is ongoing, as new information is added to the database each time new manuals are added to the collection.
Project length:	Ongoing
Cost:	Student labor was used; the software and hardware were already owned

Name:	**Electronic Song Index**
Library:	Mishawaka-Penn Public Library
Contact:	Dennis C. Tucker
Address:	Dennis C. Tucker, 6202 Morenci Tr., Indianapolis, IN 46268
Phone:	(317) 298-6570
E-mail:	Dennis@palni.edu
Hardware:	IBM PC compatible
Software:	PC-File
Description:	Whenever a patron asked at the reference desk for the lyrics to a certain song or the name of the composer, the reference staff would refer to a paper index kept for that purpose. For years the library had indexed its collection of songs on paper slips. The job was labor intensive and, of course, never up-to-date. It was necessary to convert the library's paper index of song titles to an electronic index and add new titles.

48   *Indexing*

It was decided to convert the index to an electronic format using the electronic database program PC-File. A database file was set up with fields for song title, first line, composer's name, and the title and the call number of the book containing the song. A student staff member keyed the contents of the paper file into the database. The initial data entry was somewhat time-consuming but not terribly so because the hard part (the indexing) had already been done.

The project is ongoing, as new information is added to the database each time a new songbook is added to the collection; each new songbook is given to a data-entry operator who creates new entries for the electronic index by going through the book page by page and adding each song. The index is stored on the local area network and can be accessed from any workstation on the system. The database requires a password so that data cannot be changed by unauthorized parties.

Project length: Ongoing
Cost: Student labor was used; the library already owned the software and hardware

Name: **In-House Song Index**
Library: Eisenhower Public Library
Contact: Lee Leibik
Address: 4652 N. Olcott, Harwood Heights, IL 60646
Phone: (708) 867-7828
E-mail: leibikl@sls.lib.il.us
Hardware: IBM compatible
Software: Microsoft Word, WordPad, HTML editor
Description: The song index to the library's songbook collection was compiled using Microsoft Word. The index is arranged alphabetically by song title; three-letter codes are used as abbreviations for the songbooks, which are listed in a separate file with their call numbers attached. A staff member later merges these two files into one so only one listing is used to look up the song and locate it. Because not every SWAN entry (the Suburban Library System's online catalog) lists the entire contents of every songbook, it was necessary to have a separate index. This has been a great time-saver for searching. The indexing is done during desk time.
Project length: Ongoing

Indexing **49**

Name:	**Local-Paper Obituary Index**
Library:	Eisenhower Public Library
Contact:	Lee Leibik
Address:	4652 N. Olcott, Harwood Heights, IL 60646
Phone:	(708) 867-7828
E-mail:	leibikl@sls.lib.il.us
Hardware:	IBM PC compatible
Software:	Microsoft Word
Description:	The local-paper obituary index is an alphabetical index to obituaries from the local *Norridge-Harwood Heights News* (previously titled *The Review* and *The Citizen*). It is stored on Microsoft Word. The file includes the name of the deceased individual, the date of the newspaper in which the obituary appeared, and the date of death. The file indexes obituaries from 1940 to one year prior to the present month. This file, although useful and unique to the library, is not used as much as the song index and is not always up to date because of staff labor shortages, etc.
Project length:	Ongoing

Name:	**Mel Tierney American Legion Post Digitization Project**
Library:	Park Ridge Public Library
Contact:	Anna Yackle
Address:	20 S. Prospect Ave., Park Ridge, IL 60068
Phone:	(847) 825-3123
E-mail:	ayackleb@park-ridge.lib.il.us
Hardware:	Compaq Presario, View Sonic Professional Series P775 monitor, AGFA Arcus II scanner
Software:	Adobe Pagemaker
Description:	The purpose of this project was to make available to the people of Park Ridge, genealogists, and historians digitized images of 4×6 index cards and newspaper articles regarding approximately 1,875 individuals from Park Ridge who enlisted in the service during World War II. The project has been very successful and relatively pain free so far. The one mistake made was when it was thought that funding would be available for staff through the grant. It was learned only later this was not the case, but the project would be worth doing again.
Reference:	http://www.nsn.org:2000
Project length:	July 1998–June 1999
Cost:	Equipment was purchased by North Suburban Library System using State Grant money; projected total cost is $8,000 to $12,000 in staff salaries

Name:	***Saskatchewan News* Index**
Library:	University of Saskatchewan Libraries
Contact:	Darlene Fichter
Address:	215–116 Research Dr., Saskatoon, SK Canada S7N 3R3
Phone:	(306) 966-7209
E-mail:	Darlene.Fichter@usask.ca
Hardware:	486 computers, Pentium computers, Hewlett Packard four-color scanner
Software:	HTML Assistant Pro, Microsoft Word, OmniPage Pro, WS_FTP
Description:	The *Saskatchewan News* index project provides access to newspaper stories that have been published in Saskatchewan newspapers. It involved digitizing the print indexes to Saskatchewan newspapers and merging the records with electronic indexes of more recent years. The print indexes cover the period from 1883 to 1986 and have been compiled and created by a number of agencies using different indexing rules and practices. Print indexes of good quality were scanned and optical character recognition (OCR) software was used.

It is important to scan and fine tune the OCR to achieve the best results. The quality of the mimeographed pages of some indexes was poor and most could not be scanned. Unless the accuracy rates are very high as the result of the OCR testing, it is simply faster to type the entries. A template was developed in Microsoft Word using several macros to minimize the typing required.

One of the most time-consuming and important aspects of the project was mapping over the various indexing practices from the variety of sources to an electronic index. One of the critical decisions involved obituaries. Later indexes had separate obituary indexes. Before the mid-1900s obituaries were simply included with the articles indexed under a heading "obituary." In the late 1800s and early 1900s obituaries often appeared as part of a society column. At one point the creation of a separate obituary index from 1883 to the present was considered. Given the inconsistent nature of reporting in the newspapers and the different application of indexing rules by the various indexers, this approach was not feasible.

In the process of digitization, several errors in the original indexing came to light. A policy of whether these errors will be corrected needs to be determined at the onset of the project. For example, a word in an article title may be mistyped. Was this the error of the original typist for the indexer or is this an error that first occurred in the newspaper itself? What rules were followed in the index—are typographic errors in the original articles retained in the index? For this project, it was decided to duplicate the print indexes as accurately as possible and not to try to enhance upon the original citations. This decision was made on a philosophical basis but also was very practical. With more than 700,000 citations, it was not feasible to look up every article containing suspect words or typography.

Reference:	http://library.usask.ca
Project length:	1992–1999
Cost:	Approximately $250,000 from various heritage and youth employment grants

Interlibrary Loan

The two projects in this category speed interlibrary loan delivery using microcomputers. Coastal Bend Health Information Network obtains information for health care professionals who must have quick access to requested information. Its project uses several technologies to provide this access. The Klinck Memorial Library uses the Internet to distribute Web-based interlibrary loan forms to its patrons.

Name:	**Coastal Bend Health Information Network**
Library:	Consortium of Texas A&M University–Corpus Christi, Texas A&M University–Kingsville, Del Mar College, Coastal Bend College, Spohn Memorial Hospital, Spohn Shoreline Hospital, Columbia Bay Area Medical Center, and Driscoll
Contact:	Sally Gibson, project librarian, Coastal Bend Health Network
Address:	6300 Ocean Dr., Corpus Christi, TX 78412
Phone:	(512) 994-2766
E-mail:	sgibson@falcon.tamucc.edu
Hardware:	Pentium computer, Hewlett Packard LaserJet printer, fax machine, Internet connection for each location
Software:	Microsoft Windows 95, Health Reference Center, Ovid's Medical Collection (MEDLINE, Cinahl, HealthStar, Nursing Collection, Core Biomedical Collection)
Description:	Coastal Bend Health Information Network (CBHIN) was created to provide an infrastructure for the electronic delivery of medical information to cooperating libraries. The first step was to create a union list of serials to share with members.

At the center of the system is a library assistant at Spohn Memorial Hospital. This staff member has the dual roles of providing interlibrary loan service to the CBHIN members and assisting Nursing and Allied Health students with database use.

Interlibrary loan requests are sent to the library assistant. After the journal article has been located in the Coastal Bend area, it is faxed to the requesting party. CBHIN members are given top priority. Requests are often faxed within the hour or 24 hours if marked rush. Items not available in the Coastal Bend area are sent to a full-service document delivery provider for five-day service.

This project is useful because it provides medical information in a timely manner to medical providers. The databases are full text. The key to maintaining the service is having good equipment with repair options in place at each location. Some of the problems reported were a wide variance in experience with the Internet and the World Wide Web among institutions, no conformity of computer equipment or software bought for CBHIN members, and no clear policies established about procedures for interlibrary loan.

Reference:	1997 ALA Poster Session
Project length:	1996–present
Cost:	$450,000 for three years

Name:	**Web-Based Interlibrary Loan Forms**
Library:	Klinck Memorial Library, Concordia University
Contact:	Kurt I. Munson
Address:	7400 Augusta St., River Forest, IL 60305
Phone:	(708) 209-3050
E-mail:	crflibrary@crf.cuis.edu
Hardware:	Web server
Software:	Web browsers that can support forms, HTML editor, Web server software
Description:	This project allowed students to submit interlibrary loan forms when off campus. To do so, Web-based interlibrary loan forms were created. The paper form was converted to a simple HTML-based form. Each line on the paper form was converted to a field in a Web-based form with a hidden identifier to display in the submitted request. Completed forms are e-mailed to the interlibrary loan address. A mailto.exe program in the same directory on the server facilitates sending the completed form. Hidden lines in the form add the library's fax number, address, and areas for staff use to the request as it is e-mailed so that the printed e-mail can be faxed directly to a library that owns the item.
Project length:	August 1997–present
Cost:	None

The Internet

There are many different ways to connect to the Internet, to provide Internet service to the public, and to create a Web site. An online library Web presence can provide many information services and opportunities for the public and staff. General information (such as policies, newsletters, and services), access to staff via e-mail, and links to other library sites around the world can be included. A Web site can also be a front end to a library's online public access catalog. Patrons may search the catalog and then call the library to request a hold be placed on a book.

Configurations vary, of course. Some libraries create their own Web sites, and others group together in clusters or go through an organization such as LincolnNet, which serves as a front end for local governments and municipalities. Going it alone means locating and negotiating with a service to provide access to the Web. The library's information is stored on the provider's server.

Taking a course in HTML (HyperText Markup Language) and Web site construction is a good idea. While anyone can create and upload Web pages and information to a server, a class or workshop can save an enormous amount of time.

Design of a Web site—how it looks and works—is an important aspect of the whole project. A consultant can be hired to do the entire setup and maintenance for any Web site. Surfing the Web, particularly looking at other existing library sites, can provide many ideas for design. Prior to construction, however, a survey or study should be conducted by staff to determine the extent and type of information the library wishes to place online. An elaborate Web site with complicated database availability may require the hiring of a consultant to assist with technical problems and details. This is especially true if the library puts an online public access catalog (OPAC) or another database up for patrons to search on the Web.

Librarians preparing to start a Web site should examine the St. Joseph County Public Library Web site at http://sjcpl.lib.in.us and the Chicago Public Library Internet site at http://cpl.lib.uic.edu/cpl.html for a good example of what can be done. Also, check out the site U.S. Public Libraries with Web Sites for examples at www.capecod.net/epl/public.libraries.html. At this location you'll find website design guidelines for public libraries that contains a basic public library checklist—items or links that should be considered for inclusion on Web pages. This checklist can save a lot of time brainstorming, since it includes items such as mission statement, library card policy, a virtual tour with pictures, FAQs, special collections, and many items that might be overlooked. Many ideas on Web page design using experimentation and common principles are included.

The Ablah Library (Wichita State University) has created its own special indexes or search engines for searching Internet information from two library databases, one on classics and medieval studies and one on Kansas history. The Maywood Public Library uses Electric Library through the Internet to locate information of all types from a huge Internet database of more than three million documents for general use and for student papers.

Many libraries now offer access to the Internet as a public service. A few of these ventures are related as parts of other projects elsewhere in this book (for example, see the Maywood Public Library's LAN project). The Chicago Public Library has one of the largest projects. Internet access is available at many branch libraries and at the Harold Washington Library Center. The La Grange Public Library has made two computers available, one for adult services and one for children's services. An Internet use policy was created as part of the project. The Library Online Information Service (LOIS) is a two-year British project that served as a model for future services. In that project twelve terminals provided a variety of government information to local communities.

Name:	**Building Accessibility to Technology**
Library:	La Grange Public Library
Contact:	Steve Moskal
Address:	10 W. Cossitt Ave., La Grange, IL 60525
Phone:	(708) 352-0576
E-mail:	moskals@sls.lib.il.us
Hardware:	Adtran DSU, Micom 5000, IRM router module, Network Card
Software:	Netscape Navigator 3.0, Fortres 101
Description:	The goal of this project was to provide Internet access to the patrons of the La Grange Public Library. Two workstations were created, one in the adult services department and one in the youth services department. The public response to the program has been very positive. The library continues to maintain the hardware and software even after the end of the official grant term. It was necessary to create an Internet use policy that is posted on the library's Web site.
Reference:	www.lagrangeil.com/lgs
Project length:	Ongoing
Cost:	$9,565 ($5,261 from local funds; $4,304 from an LSCA Title II Technology)

Name:	**Chicago Public Library Internet Access**
Library:	The Chicago Public Library
Address:	400 S. State St., Chicago, IL 60605
Hardware:	IBM PC compatible
Software:	Netscape Navigator 3.01
Description:	The Chicago Public Library serves millions of Chicago residents and provides reciprocal borrowing and services to surrounding communities and to the State of Illinois. Internet access is available at many branches and locations. Most have only one computer, which can create occasional problems. Users are warned that there may be inappropriate or inaccurate information on the Internet and that the library cannot be held responsible for these problems. The grant application for the project is online at http://www.chipublib.org/003cpl/lscagrant.html. Information about public Internet use at the Chicago Public Library is at http:www.chipublib.org/003cpl/internet/about.html.

A pilot project was funded through the Illinois State Library LSCA grant that provided public Internet services to the Harold Washington Library Center, regional libraries, and some branch libraries.

A local branch library, the Logan Square Branch Library, has one Internet computer available for the public. There, up to two one-half hour appointments to use the computer may be made by telephone. The computer is located in the center of the adult reference and reading room so that viewing by passers-by is ensured to inhibit any X-rated uses of the computer. The service is fast and provides complete Web access without filtering. The staff has put together a good "Internet Computer Rules" for the Logan Square Branch stating the hours during which the service is available. Any person may use the Internet for a maximum of one and one-half hours per week. Printing is permitted but only three pictures during any visit. I had no trouble getting an appointment within thirty minutes of my first call. The librarian on duty said that there had been few problems. Only one person—a youth—had knowingly tried to download adult-related pictures. The rules also state that computers may be used only for information purposes—no games allowed.

Project length:	July 1, 1994–present

Name:	**Computer Tutors Put Vets on the Net**
Library:	Ashland Public Library
Contacts:	Debra Aggertt; Lori Bell

Address:	Debra Aggertt, Ashland Public Library District, 125 W. Editor, P.O. Box 498, Ashland, IL 62612
Phone:	(217) 476-3417; Fax: (217) 476-8076
E-mail:	ashl@darkstar.rsa.lib.il.us
Address:	Lori Bell, Alliance Library System, 845 Brenkman Dr., Pekin, IL 61554
Phone:	(800) 700-4857
E-mail:	lbell@darkstar.rsa.lib.il.us
Hardware:	IBM PC 486, modem
Software:	HTML for creating Web pages
Description:	The computer tutors put vets on the net project resulted in young adults and armed forces veterans participating in the creation of a home page and shared training, ideas, and experiences through the Internet using a variety of methods such as e-mail, a discussion list created for this project, and a home page at www.rsa.lib.il/us~sedward/vets/resource.html. This created an innovative model for intergenerational programming that involved adults and senior citizens.

Six libraries participated. Each recruited five young adults who were trained on the Internet through a workshop and a training course. They were then responsible for training five veterans on the Internet who also participated in the online training course.

A significant problem to be resolved was the recruitment of veterans to participate. Also, local libraries should have been involved sooner, scheduling time for the students to work with the veterans.

The Ashland Public Library District staff learned a great deal from the project. They increased their knowledge of the use of the Internet and its capabilities, developed an understanding of the design of Web pages, and learned how to deal with two different segments of the same community. It also brought in many new library users. |
Reference:	Arlia Dittmer, "Computer Tutors Put Vets on the Net," *Illinois Libraries* Vol. 80, no. 1 (Winter 1998): 32.
Project length:	October 1996–June 1997
Cost:	$23,780, LSCA project funded by the Secretary of State/Illinois State Library

Name:	**Developing an Internet Workshop Using a Class Home Page**
Library:	Tennessee State Library and Archives
Contact:	Charles A. Sherrill

Address:	403 7th Ave. N., Nashville, TN 37243-0312
Phone:	(615) 741-2764; Fax: (615) 532-2472
E-mail:	csherrill@mail.state.tn.us
Hardware:	IBM PC compatible classroom network, 1 PC for each student
Software:	Microsoft Word 6.0, HTML editor, Netscape Navigator
Description:	The library sponsored a hands-on Internet workshop for beginners that showed a group of 25 students the most interesting and useful sites for researching genealogy (but this would work using any topic). The class was held in a computer lab in a community college. A simple but appealing Web page was developed that listed all of the links to be reviewed, including a brief description of the value of each link. This page was mounted on the library's Web site. Just before the class began, the browsers on all the computers in the lab were reset so that this became the "home" page for those terminals during the class. Students clicked through these links and discussed each page in turn. When the class was over, all students were given the URL for the "home" page, and left it up for a couple of months so that they could use it from their homes as a starting point for learning to use the Web.

Developing this page worked out very well both as an instructional tool and as an aid for class members' later reference. It took two or three hours to develop and test, and it cost nothing beyond staff time. The class is offered periodically, and updating the page is a simple matter of testing the old links and adding new ones. |
Reference:	http://www.state.tn.us/gos/statelib/pubsvs/find-if.htm
Project length:	Quarterly classes from spring 1998–present
Cost:	None

Name:	**Harvest Server**
Library:	Ablah Library, Wichita State University
Contact:	Brian Hancock
Address:	1845 Fairmount, Wichita, KS 67260-0068
Phone:	(316) 978-5077; Fax: (316) 978-3048
E-mail:	bhancock@loca.ablah.twsu.edu
Hardware:	Alpha PC 164XL, 533 MHZ, 128 K RAM
Software:	Linux 5.1, Harvest Information Discovery and Access System 1.5.20
Description:	This project has currently set up two subject-specific search engines: Index Antiquus and the Kansas History Index. Both may be found at http://harvest.ablah.twsu.edu. The Index Antiquus is an index for classics and medieval studies. Using the Harvest

system, users may search for any terms and specify various options, such as case insensitive, keywords match on word boundaries, number of spelling errors allowed, Boolean logic, etc. The gatherer (a Harvest feature) is sent out to the World Wide Web to retrieve information from sites deemed relevant by a librarian. These sites are evaluated with certain criteria such as authoritativeness, accuracy, recency of data, appropriateness, relevancy, organization, and stability. To keep the information current, the gatherer is sent out periodically to gather new information from sites.

The system is maintained by the humanities librarian but is quite automated and now requires little intervention by staff. Anyone who is interested in setting up such a system is invited to contact the system administration.

References:	Brian Hancock, "Subject-Specific Search Engines," *Library Software Review* (June 1998): 84–89.
	http://wwwharvest.ablah.twsu.edu
Project length:	January 1998–present
Cost:	$4,414 for hardware; software free

Name:	**Kent County Library System Information Kiosk**
Library:	Kent County Library
Contact:	Richard L. Krueger
Address:	414 Federal St., Dover, DE 19901
Phone:	(302) 736-2265; Fax: (302) 736-2262
E-mail:	krueger@kentnet.dtcc.edu
Hardware:	Public Information Kiosk
Software:	PI Kiosk
Description:	The Kent County Department of Library Services is responsible for providing the automated library system for the public libraries in Kent County. The county also operates a bookmobile for the rural areas around the capital of Dover. From this outreach service came the idea of a library information kiosk. With Dover as the center of Kent County, most people living in the rural areas come into the city periodically to shop. They do not find their way into the downtown area with its parking problems and thus avoid visiting the Dover Public Library. Because the Dover Mall is away from the center of downtown and has major stores, people from all over Delaware shop there. With this in mind, the library decided that the kiosk should be an avenue for those individuals with limited access to a library (even a bookmobile) or a home computer. The focus was on library services

(locating and requesting library materials) and information sources available through the automated library system (KentNet) such as online full-text periodicals. The kiosk is an ideal way of reaching people with information about government services.

It should be noted that a library kiosk that simply provides information about libraries or government services will never have the draw of an automated bank machine. The approach was to provide limited access to high-interest Internet sites. Something was needed to attract those who were walking by to stop at the kiosk. It took a great deal of time to select interesting Internet sites.

The monthly usage statistics provided by Public Information Kiosks, Inc., are a valuable component in maintaining a high interest kiosk. In the first year of operation, the kiosk has had more than 4,000 touches on the screen per month. The touch screen of the Kiosk permits the most timid of individuals with limited or no computer skills to use the resource. For the month of August 1998, there were 4,361 touches on the kiosk. Of this number, the most popular were Blue Rocks baseball, Dover Downs Race Track, local beach information, job opportunities, and the mall directory. What is interesting is that the KentNet card catalog has had more than any of these touches except the mall directory. A few people now request books by placing them on hold at the kiosk, and the following day they go to one of the libraries in the KentNet to pick them up.

It is advisable to form a development team for the kiosk to decide who will be responsible for monitoring and updating the Web sites. Keeping good sites and changing them periodically makes the kiosk a dynamic attraction.

In the first three months, there was a problem with the ISDN line that was finally corrected. The kiosk has continued to run smoothly with minimal staff involvement. It is important, however, to have someone check on the kiosk every few days to determine if there are problems or if it needs cleaning. Shopping malls may provide basic cleaning around the kiosk; however, they should not be depended upon to keep the kiosk clean for public use.

Project length: Ongoing; one year to plan and install
Cost: Kiosk, $37,500; phone installation, $450; mall rent, $1,400 per year; vendor kiosk maintenance, approximately $6,200; service maintenance, $7,700 yearly

Name:	**Library Online Information Service (LOIS)**
Library:	Worcestershire Libraries and Information Service
Contact:	David Drewitt, principal librarian
Address:	Information Services, Libraries and Information Service, County Hall, Spetchley Rd., Worcester WR5 2NP, England
E-mail:	ddrewitt@worcestershire.gov.uk
Hardware:	Dell computers, NT servers, 12 standard high-specification PCs as terminals, leased British Telecom lines and communications equipment
Description:	This large project was designed to improve the "penetration of community centres with hard copy sources of information," and to "improve contact with people in rural areas." It carries public community information to computer terminals in public libraries, council offices, and a village hall/post office in a rural community. The information includes county and district council information (contact details, services, departments, meetings, reports, and so on), tourist information, information from voluntary bodies, lists of clubs and societies, county council job vacancies, databases of rail timetables, and other government information.

The community information is held on a server at County Hall, Worcester, linked to the terminals by 64 K leased lines that are currently shared by the county libraries' cataloging, membership, and issue system. District councils' (currently South Herefordshire DC and Hereford City Council) networks are connected to LOIS.

Lessons learned during the project led to the establishment at the end of the project (1995) of LOIS (Library Online Information Service) as an ongoing service provided entirely by Libraries Service within the county. It is now available in terminals in main libraries throughout the county, in some district council offices, in two council information shops, and for staff through desktop PCs in County Hall. Soon to be expanded by linking with the main library system, LOIS will be available in all 32 libraries through the library's OPACs and catalog and borrowers' services also available through LOIS. It is accessible on Internet at http://www.worcestershire.gov.uk.

LOIS proper is an Intranet, although it looks and behaves in a way similar to the Internet, using Web page format and hot links. However, LOIS is the county council's presence on the Internet and is the authorized Web site for the county council. External Internet users can view all of the LOIS databases, although it would be possible to deny access to some or to control access by password. The LOIS servers act as a gateway to the Internet for authorized users (using terminals on the County Hall network) on County Hall business; the possibility of using this link for other users will be considered when data on Internet usage and the consequent load on communications has been assessed.

Users of public LOIS terminals in libraries and other venues have access to designated databases on the Internet. These are "public information" databases with access controlled by the server holding lists of "nonpermitted" databases. The user will not be able to access databases on the lists to reduce the possibility of users accessing, for example, pornographic sites. The possibility of general access to the Internet will be considered separately. It is likely that general Internet access will use terminals other than LOIS terminals and may well be charged for, unlike the "directed" access through LOIS, which will remain free to the user and will be subject to an "acceptable use" policy.

By acting pragmatically, the goal is a dispersed community information system, easy to use and update, with information providers "owning" their own information and being responsible for providing updates. This two-year project was considered a success and led to the eventual formation of LOIS. According to accounts, setup time was much longer than anticipated.

Reference:	Sarah Ormes and Lorcan Dempsey, eds., *The Internet, Networking and the Public Library* (London, Eng.: Library Association Publishing, 1997).
Project length:	1993–present

Name:	**LIBSTATS: Library Statistics on the Web**
Library:	Northern Illinois University Libraries
Contact:	Elizabeth A. Titus, associate professor
Address:	136 FML, Northern Illinois University, De Kalb, IL 60115
Phone:	(815) 753-9701
E-mail:	etlives@niu.edu
Hardware:	Web page server
Software:	Quattro Pro for Windows; Microsoft Word HTML; Quarterdeck Web Server 1
Description:	LIBSTATS, Library statistics on the Web site, was designed to share local, state, national, and foreign library statistical reports electronically; provide examples of the library statistics being reported; promote the use of library statistics; and provide information on other Web sites dealing with library statistics data gathering and reporting. It provides wide access to library statis-

tics for both internal and external use. Internally, it provides direct access to data on a timely basis by library staff for decision making and reporting purposes. Externally, it provides a way to promote libraries and to demonstrate the variety of library services offered locally, regionally, and statewide.

Suggestions for those who may want to try this type of project include making statistical information more interesting by using graphics such as bar charts, pie charts, and maps. Next, when reporting statistics, it is important to keep the data as current as possible. Finally, reporting statistics electronically is a cost-effective way to reach a broader audience and to publish this type of information.

References: Elizabeth Titus "Library Statistics: Trends in Electronic Data Reporting on the Web," in *Computers in Libraries '98: Proceedings of the 13th Annual Computers in Libraries Conference* (Medford, N.J.: Information Today, 1998).
http://131.156.59.13/etst.htm
Project length: 1994–present
Cost: Internal library operating budget

Name: **Park Ridge Community Network NorthStar:**
A North Suburban Library System NorthStarNet Project
Library: Park Ridge Public Library
Contact: Kathy Rolsing
Address: 20 S. Prospect Ave., Park Ridge, IL 60068
Phone: (847) 825-3123 x202
E-mail: krolsing@park-ridge.lib.il.us
Hardware: Windows NT network with Pentium staff computers; digital camera, scanner; PIK Information Kiosk
Software: HTML Assistant Pro 97, Microsoft Internet Explorer, Netscape Communicator
Description: The Park Ridge Community Network is an online resource with a wide range of information about community events, school activities and curricula, municipal services, cultural programs, and library services. The network is brought to the community by the Park Ridge Public Library and NorthStarNet (NSN), the regional information network of the North Suburban Library System offering information about more than 40 neighboring suburbs.

The Park Ridge Public Library coordinates the Park Ridge Community Network, which is maintained by community information providers including the city of Park Ridge, Community

Consolidated School District #64, Maine Township High School District #207, and the Park Ridge Recreation and Park District as well as 60 additional community organizations, churches, and businesses. Each provider designs and maintains its own site using its own equipment, but providers may also use the library's dedicated NSN computer, scanner, and digital camera for development of their sites. Through the library, providers may also contract with local high school student designers to develop Web pages.

Information may be accessed through home or office computers, through Internet stations in the library, or through the electronic touch-screen kiosk located at the Park Ridge Recreation and Park District Community Center. The kiosk offers access to the entire NorthStarNet site and all associated links.

This successful project has been very well received by the community and staff at the library. It is recommended that the community organizations be involved from the beginning and that each organization be responsible for its own site rather than depending on the library, for example, to design pages for it. The creation of a community advisory committee is also a good idea. All important decisions can be addressed at that committee rather than having decisions and policies made by one individual for the entire community.

References:	Park Ridge Community Network: http://www.park-ridge.il.us
	NorthStarNet: http://www.northstarnet.org
Project length:	May 31, 1996–present
Cost:	40 percent of staff members' time at a cost of $13,000 annually and other additional resources including hardware and software as indicated; community organizations fund the staff time necessary to maintain their portions of the community site; funds come from the library's operating budget; one computer and scanner were received through a partnership between the North Suburban Library System and the Chicago Tribune Digital City project; the kiosk was purchased through an LSCA grant from the State of Illinois

Name:	**St. Joseph County Public Library Internet Use**
Library:	St. Joseph County Public Library
Address:	304 S. Main St., South Bend, IN 46661
Phone:	(219) 282-4630
Hardware:	T-1 line, leased 56/64 KB lines
Description:	St. Joseph County Public Library has pioneered Web site con-

struction for public libraries and for in-house use of the Internet by patrons. It is a good model from which other libraries may work. The main page provides access to the library's OPAC, a community information search page, a local newspaper search page, necrology search page, a public library server search page, and an infofile. Information about the library and its departments, branches, policies, volunteer and job opportunities, programs, what's new, and much more can be readily reached from the first page. Just about every service at the library is described in detail. Patrons can e-mail library employees to offer suggestions or to ask for more information. Computer classes at the library are listed.

The library offers introductory and advanced classes on Internet use at the library by someone well versed in the Internet. Furthermore, the library has a well thought-out plan for reaching the public and providing Internet services. For example, there is an online page called "My rules for online safety," that outlines how to avoid getting into trouble on the Internet (aimed at children) by not giving out personal information, etc. There is also a reprint of "Child Safety on the Information Highway" (National Center for Missing and Exploited Children and Interactive Services Association) online. This lengthy document gives parents basic information about the benefits, risks, and how to use cyberspace responsibly and safely. Another article is called "Internet at the St. Joseph County Public Library...a brief history." This 1,000-word document gives an overview of how these projects began.

Staff training, as reported in this article, was an enormous problem. Training sessions first proceeded with the main library public service staff (except circulation staff). Each person received three sessions of three hours each on Internet use. Branch staff then received two two-hour sessions of training that included hands-on experience using five Macintosh computers in a special training room. When enough staff had been trained to make everyone feel comfortable, the job of providing the Internet to the public was undertaken.

The first installation consisted of three computers grouped together in what was called "The Internet Connection." Since Notre Dame was already established as an Internet node, all that the library had to provide was a 56 KB leased line to go from the library to Notre Dame. It paid a one-time startup fee to CirNet in Ann Arbor, Michigan, its network provider. As of December 1995, an upgrade converted the line to a T-1 and linked branch libraries directly to the main network through 56/64 KB lines. Three cluster libraries (Mishawaka Public Library, Plymouth Public Library, and Bremen Public Library) joined the network with direct 56/64 KB lines.

Reference: http://sjcpl.lib.in.us/
Project length: Ongoing
Cost: Leased line, $237 per month; to CirNet for Net maintenance, $4,500 per year

Name: **Scout Report for Science and Engineering, Scout Report for Business and Economics, Scout Report for Social Sciences**
Organization: Computer Sciences Department, University of Wisconsin–Madison
Contact: Jack Solock
Address: 1210 W. Dayton St., Madison, WI 53706
Phone: (608) 262-6606
E-mail: jacks@cs.wisc.edu
Hardware: Sun SPARC 4 and Power Macintosh
Software: Excite, FileMaker Pro for Windows, Apache, WebSTAR
Description: Scout Report is a current-awareness reader advisory service designed to track, evaluate, and disseminate news of new information resources on the Internet. Scout Report has been in continuous publication since 1994. It is a weekly newsletter that evaluates and annotates Internet resources in research and education, general interest fields, and network tools. In 1997, three subject-specific Scout Reports produced by librarians and subject specialists began publication (Scout Report for Science and Engineering, Scout Report for Social Sciences, and the Scout Report for Business and Economics). The addition of the subject-specific Scout Reports has allowed for more-selective dissemination of information to subscribers since it filters and organizes Internet information according to subject area.

Each Scout Report attempts to provide evaluations for a balance of resources, including full-text books, journals, metasites, and other sites of interest. In addition to the announcement of new resources, subject-specific Scout Reports contain announcements of conferences, electronic publications, grant and job information, and the release of working papers specific to the subject area. To find new Internet resources, editors monitor some 200 discussion lists, Usenet news groups, and major newspapers; search the Internet and metasites; and receive submissions from readers. Items are selected for the Scout Reports based on contents, authority, information maintenance, presentation, availability, and cost (emphasis is on freely available resources).

Each Scout Report is free and freely available in weekly or bimonthly compilations via e-mail or on the Internet Scout Project Web site. Each Scout Report provides people with a means to quickly and conveniently become informed about new, quality information that has been published on the Internet in their subject area without having to spend a significant amount of time and energy monitoring new sites.

It is important to develop a newsprint for consistency and formatting at the outset of such a project. It is recommended that a style guide be developed to maintain editorial consistency.

References:	Susan Calcari and Jack Solock, "The Internet Scout Project: Filtering for Quality," *Choice* 34 (supplement 1997): 25–30.
	Jack Solock, "Anatomy of a Scout Report: Resource Discovery in the Information Age, or How We Do It," *End Users' Corner* (Mar. 1997). Available at http://scout.cs.wisc.edu.scout.toolkit.enduser/archive/1997/euc-9606.html
	Jack Solock, "Site-ation Pearl Growing," *End Users' Corner* (June 1996). Available at http://scout.cs.wisc.edu/scout/toolkit/enduser/archive/1996/euc-9606.html
Project length:	1994–2000
Cost:	$250,000 per year from National Science Foundation

Name:	**Scout Report Research and Development**
Organization:	Computer Sciences Department, University of Wisconsin–Madison
Contact:	Susan Calcari
Address:	1210 W. Dayton St., Madison, WI 53706
Phone:	(608) 265-8042
E-mail:	scal@cs.wisc.edu
Hardware:	Sun SPARC 4 and Power Macintosh
Software:	Excite, FileMaker Pro for Windows, Apache, WebSTAR
Description:	This project was developed to advance the discovery of Internet resources in the research and educational fields and to serve as a test bed for more-sophisticated, next-generation protocols, databases, and directory service technologies. Since the funding source for this project is the Advanced Networking and Infrastructure Research Division (ANIR) of the National Science Foundation (NSF), the goals have been to improve the level of knowledge and access to networked information, especially with regard to the research and education community in the United States.

As the amount of information on the Internet has grown, it has become more difficult for individual researchers and educators to stay current with the resources available in specific fields. To this end, the Internet Scout Project employs subject specialists, educators, librarians, and computer scientists to focus on the areas of selective dissemination of information (SDI) and network tools. SDI is accomplished by way of the Scout Reports, regularly published newsletters that evaluate and annotate Internet resources. Net-Happenings is a discussion group and Web site that identifies new Internet resources, publications, and conferences on a daily basis. The K.I.D.S. Report is an annotated newsletter that offers reviews of quality Internet sites by and for school-aged children. Network Tools is another newsletter. It includes the Scout Report Toolkit, which includes information on specific Internet resources and the tools database of Scout Report summaries, and Isaac, a search engine that seeks to unite information from all participating collections.

A visit to the Scout Project Web site is the best way to understand it. The main page has a variety of services, including the newsletter, the Signpost database, and other services. From the main page, a quick search can be made by entering the topic desired. A more-refined search can be made with the advanced search page using Boolean logic and a variety of search terms. There is also a browse by subject headings function that currently lists 1,980 report summaries by topic.

Each report has a 100- to 200-word abstract available. From this abstract readers may obtain the purpose of the Web site, its goals, and its intended audience. Users can also browse by Library of Congress classifications. These group LC categories into a variety of subject headings, such as music, law, bibliography and library, language and literature, history, social sciences, etc.

While this is not a project that most libraries can undertake, it is certainly one that most can access for their own patrons and work. A big problem for its developers has been the rapid growth of the project and growth of the Internet. Due to the rapid expansion of the Internet, it is suggested by the project coordinators that future projects in these areas focus on core, closely interrelated issues in networked information.

References: A.T. Wells, Susan Carcari, and Jack Solock, "The Internet Scout Project," *Library Hi Tech* 15, no. 3–4 (1997): 11–18.

Susan Calcari and Jack Solock, "The Internet Scout Project: Filtering for Quality," *Choice* 34 (supplement 1997): 25–30.

Karen G. Schneider, "Scouting for Net Sites," *American Libraries* 28, no. 7 (Aug. 1997): 88.

Teri Boomsma, "Site Management Solutions of the Internet Scout Project," *End Users' Corner* (Sept. 1997). Available at http://scout.cs.wisc.edu/scout/toolkit/enduser/archive/1997/euc-9709.html

Project length: Funded March 1997–April 2000
Cost: $250,000 from National Science Foundation

Name: **Scout Report Signpost**
Organization: Computer Sciences Department, University of Wisconsin–Madison
Contact: Amy Tracy Wells
Address: 1210 W. Dayton St., Madison, WI 53706
Phone: (608) 263-2611
E-mail: awells@cs.wisc.edu
Hardware: Sun SPARC 4 and Power Macintosh
Software: Excite, FileMaker Pro for Windows, Apache, WebSTAR
Description: Signpost is a search-and-browse Internet database that contains descriptive summaries of more than 4,000 Internet sites evaluated and annotated in the Scout Reports, a series of regularly published newsletters. Four catalogers are working toward the goal of cataloging and classifying all Signpost records according to the Dublin Core metadata standards, utilizing Library of Congress Subject Headings and the Library of Congress classification scheme. LC classification was chosen because it is a widely recognized taxonomy in the research and education community. Other schemes are being explored as well. A major problem was the development of semantic and syntactic cataloging standards for Internet resources.

Approximately 2,000 of these records have been cataloged using traditional and emerging standards with the Library of Congress Subject Headings and the Dublin Core metadata standards.

The overriding purpose of Signpost is to provide a refined, organized outlet for Internet resources that have been selectively chosen and evaluated by the editors of the Scout Report. Signpost adds entries at the rate of approximately 200 per month.

Internet sites are analyzed for content, subject headings, classification codes, and bibliographic information. Users of the index may search all records by keyword. Cataloged records may be searched by title, author, subject heading, publisher, resource type (for example, newspaper/journal), database, audio, etc., resource location (government, educational, commercial, etc.) or LC classification. In addition, users can browse by subject heading or classification. All links are verified once per month and updated as necessary.

Currently, many public, college, and university libraries have a link to Signpost from their Web pages. This allows library users organized access to preselected, evaluated Internet information and gives them enhanced access to Internet resources since they can search on the annotation as well as bibliographic information and subject headings.

It is suggested that people use a database to provide access to Internet resources rather than create a "meta-page" or listing of suggested Internet resources. Using a database allows users to manipulate contents for display purposes and allows subject areas to be created as needed.

References: A. T. Wells, "A Scout Report Signpost Look at One Aspect of Metadata Resource Type," *End Users' Corner* 2 no. 11 (Nov. 1997). Available at http://scout.cs.wisc.edu/scout/toolkit/archive/1997/euc-9711.html

Aimee D. Glassel and Amy Tracy Wells, "Scout Report Signpost Design and Development for Access to Cataloged Internet Resources," *Journal of Internet Cataloging* 1, no. 3 (1998): 15–45.

Additional information available at http://www.signpost.org/

Project length: Funded March 1997–April 2000
Cost: $250,000 from National Science Foundation

Name: **Staff and Patron Home Pages**
Library: Park Ridge Public Library
Contact: Brandee Crisp
Address: 20 S. Prospect Ave., Park Ridge, IL 60068
Phone: (847) 825-3123 x202
E-mail: bcrisp@park-ridge.lib.il.us
Hardware: Windows NT network with Pentium staff computers
Software: HTML Assistant Pro 97, Microsoft Internet Explorer, Netscape Communicator
Description: The Park Ridge Library's home pages provide a centralized source of helpful information and Web site links for staff and patrons. The patron site includes recommended links in more than a dozen categories, links to online subscriptions, and helpful information. The staff site has a "What's Happening in the Building" newsletter. "Library Lines" is an online newsletter for

staff. It links to online subscriptions, online demos, and other staff-oriented information.

They are both time-intensive projects that require continual and regular updates. An attempt is being made to develop a staff team to maintain and improve the sites rather than one or two staff members designing pages when time permits. The staff home page provides the information or links so they do not have to remember and type in addresses of relevant Web pages.

Reference: http://www.park-ridge.il.us
Project length: Summer 1997–present

Name: **Statement of Internet Policy on Public Access PCs**
Library: Klinck Memorial Library, Concordia University
Contact: Kurt I. Munson
Address: 7400 Augusta St., River Forest, IL 60305
Phone: (708) 209-3050
E-mail: crflibrary@crf.cuis.edu
Hardware: Public access PCs
Software: Microsoft Windows 95, Paintbrush Pro, Netscape Navigator
Description: The library uses Netscape Navigator to access databases to which the library has subscribed. To reduce the amount of entertainment Internet use at the library, which would overwhelm PC use and make it difficult to use the PCs for database access, this project's goal was to state the library's Internet use policy electronically on all public access PCs. The best, most-obvious place to post this information, it was decided, was the Windows 95 desktop. Using the Paintbrush program that comes with Windows, a background wallpaper in school colors was created that contained the full text of the policy. The file was then saved to the Windows directory, where it was used as the wallpaper.
Project length: August 1997–present
Cost: None

Name: *Treasure Island* **Web Site**
Library: UK Office for Library and Information Networking
Contact: Sarah Ormes
Address: The UK Office for Library and Information Networking, University of Bath, Bath, UK BA2 7AY
E-mail: s.l.ormes@ukoln.ac.uk
Hardware: PC, Web server
Software: HoTMetaL

Description:	The purpose of this project was to explore ways in which children's libraries could integrate the Internet into their literature-based services. This experimental Web site at http://www.ukoln.ac.uk/treasure/ will pave the way for a more advanced Web site later. The overall goal of the site is to get visitors interested enough to read the novel *Treasure Island*. The variety of areas on the site include explore *Treasure Island* (visit and explore interesting places from the book), do a book review (visitors write and send in their book reviews), answer questions in a *Treasure Island* Quiz, design a pirate (invent and send in the description of your pirate to the site), go on an online treasure hunt (The Legend of Captain Dave's Lost Treasure Chest), and access a teaching unit for *Treasure Island* (for school projects about the book).

 Treasure Island was used for this pilot project because it was out of copyright and presented no permissions problems. When the next, more sophisticated site goes up, it is expected to use at least some copyrighted (contemporary) material that will allow for participation by the author.

 Students who use the site are encouraged to both read and pick up several computer skills, such as e-mail, word processing, and the use of the Internet. There is also a text-based virtual reality system (a MOO) that is a collection of various rooms (locations) from the book. A section of links to other Web-based resources provides further information about the individual characters in the book and the author.

 To undertake a project such as this, librarians will have to have significant Web authoring skills or hire someone to do it for them. Authors of this site indicate that children enjoy the site and that it works well to promote reading. They believe that it would be even better to include higher levels of interactivity that would make it even more appealing. |
| Reference: | http://www.ariadne.ac.uk/issue6/public-libraries/ |
| Project length: | Summer 1996–present |

Name:	**Using the Electric Library as an Information Resource in a Public Library**
Library:	Maywood Public Library
Contact:	Patrick R. Dewey, director
Address:	121 S. Fifth Ave., Maywood, IL 60153
Phone:	(708) 343-1847; Fax: (708) 343-2115
E-mail:	patrickdewey@hotmail.com
Hardware:	IBM PC with Internet connection

Software:	Electric Library, Microsoft Internet Explorer
Description:	The Maywood Library recently subscribed to Electric Library, an online database of wide-ranging, popular data. It has helped to lower overall database cost from close to $20,000 per year to less than $5,000 per year. Electric Library was acquired through a special pricing made available through the suburban library system.
	The database contains more than three million documents that may be searched intuitively using Boolean logic. Any or all categories of documents (newspapers, magazines, pictures, books, etc.) may be searched as a single category or simultaneously. Browsing (that is, sequential viewing) of newspaper or magazine files or issues is not permitted. All items are available as full text, which saves sending for the material through interlibrary loan or fax. Electric Library can be accessed through Netscape Navigator or the Internet Explorer. A demo package may be obtained at its Web site at http://www.elibrary.com. The package includes separate databases for newspapers, magazines, pictures, TV and radio transcripts, and maps. Material is updated and added daily.
Project length:	1998–present
Cost:	$600 per simultaneous user through a special arrangement with the Suburban Library System

Local Area Networks, Intranets, and Cooperatives

Networking in different ways is now a common practice in libraries. Local Area Networks (LANs) allow libraries to integrate various workstations and functions. LANs are especially popular with schools and universities that need to make resources available to an entire classroom or to people scattered over a campus. Technically, a LAN consists of as few as two computers. Typically, it consists of a server and multiple client workstations. The planning for a LAN should be done with the help of a knowledgeable consultant. It also helps if some staff members are familiar with computers and LANs or at least with their capabilities and functions.

Intranets, also included in this chapter, represent an expanding use in libraries. An intranet consists of Internet technology (browsers and databases) housed on an internal company (or library) server with connections to the Internet or to other servers. The Rochester Hills Public Library created an intranet for its own internal staff use that allows for better communication and information sharing for everyone.

The Starkville High School Library has implemented a three-way cooperative involving two major universities: Mississippi State and Mississippi University for Women. The effort significantly increased the library's resources. As part of the Golden Triangle Regional Library Consortium, the students now have access to 75 computers and 2 computer labs.

Networking between larger and larger groups of libraries has become an increasingly popular and useful practice in recent years. Such networking is definitely the wave of the future.

    Name: **Developing and Planning a Local Area Network**
  Library: Maywood Public Library
  Contact: Patrick R. Dewey, director
  Address: Maywood Public Library, 121 S. Fifth Ave., Maywood, IL 60153
   Phone: (708) 343-1847; Fax: (708) 343-2115

E-mail:	patrickdewey@hotmail.com
Hardware:	Compaq server, 25 workstations, online catalog database connection, CD-ROM towers, 6 direct Internet connections
Software:	Corel Classic Literature (CD-ROM), InfoTrac databases (CD-ROM), Newsbank's *Chicago Tribune* database (CD-ROM), CollegeSource (CD-ROM), Electric Library, Cyber Patrol, Netscape Navigator, WordPerfect
Description:	The purpose of the project was to include the Internet for public use, online and CD-ROM databases, and access to the SWAN (GEAC) online catalog. Four consultants and firms were hired to complete the project. Others were hired for specific aspects of the project. During the planning stage, decisions were made about hardware (CD-ROM towers, server, workstations, etc.), cabling, and software (CD-ROMs, word processors, Internet connections, and security software). It was determined that the LAN should have 26 computers—11 for staff and 15 for public use.

The first two weeks the new library was open were the most difficult, since the system was not yet fully operational and was plagued with glitches. Eventually, most of these were worked out and stability was achieved. However, it occasionally freezes up floor by floor. Internet access created its own problems because students descended upon the PCs after school and took up every workstation to be entertained on the Internet. Since this allowed no one else to use the other resources, such as CD-ROMs, word processing, etc., it was decided to remove Netscape Navigator from all but 6 machines, at least temporarily. Two business room computers were reserved for adults only.

In addition, the Internet provided problems of appropriateness for children. It was quickly decided to install Cyber Patrol on the server to filter out various sites deemed inappropriate for children. Unfortunately, this also began to filter out sites that many adults wanted to see, even those that were appropriate for research. As a result, the filtering was removed from at least one adult workstation and warning signs were posted at this PC.

Another problem is the amount of help patrons need with various applications. While staff can help some people with some problems, most patrons must rely on their own resourcefulness or on tutorial material provided. Recently, student lab assistants have been enlisted to make appointments and to assist with basic questions, thus significantly relieving librarians.

All in all, the system works and provides enormous flexibility and many more resources over the previous stand-alone workstations. Mornings typically see many adults using the computers to create résumés, search business information, and plan projects. Between 800 and 1,000 users are seen each month compared with fewer than 100 before the LAN was instituted.

Staff use of computers has also soared. All department heads and librarians have a microcomputer near at hand now. The adult reference department has two at the reference desk. These are used to emulate the GEAC catalog (this is handy, since the budget only allowed for 11 GEAC ports for the entire library).

Present arrangements also allow for significant growth in the future if funding and the need for more computer resources become available. There are 150 actual physical locations for workstations throughout the library. Cable conduit runs to all of these, but only 100 have been data cabled and only 50 are presently in use.

The most important lesson learned was that resources require careful management, including hardware, software, and staff. A room full of computers cannot just be set up and left unmanaged —they will not get proper and adequate use without additional interventions. In the future, the library's Web site (http://www.maywood.org) will be integrated with in-house computers. Presently, the reference staff is compiling a list of library-related sites to add to a favorite-link list. Someday, when the technical details have been worked out, patrons will be allowed to access the library's online catalog through the Internet as well. Maintaining a Web site is a lot of work. Trying to do this and finish the new library at the same time has not been possible.

Project length: 1997–present
Cost: $200,000

Name: **Network System's Securities**
Library: Marywood University Library
Contact: Zhong Geng
Address: Marywood University Library, 2300 Adams Ave., Scranton, PA 18509
Phone: (570) 348-6262
Hardware: Gateway Pentium computers
Software: Menu Builder, FoolProof Desktop Security, McAfee VirusScan
Description: The library's CD-ROM network consists of several Gateway Pentium machines and can be used to access the CD-ROM resources, full-text databases, Web information, and the online catalog. To prevent library patrons from deleting files and downloading information to the hard drive, a sound security system is

highly recommended. Based on the library's situation, the combination of Menu Builder and FoolProof was used to equip the network systems with multiple security functions. Menu Builder not only facilitates the use of information resources located on the systems but it also keeps users from getting into some programs and files that are not for public use. However, in some cases, users did pass the Menu Builder's screen to access the Program Manager. FoolProof, in this situation, is set to eliminate features such as delete and exit Windows, which further protects the system. Also, FoolProof can dictate users' downloading to floppy disk rather than to the hard drive. Recently, McAfee was installed on the network to increase virus protection. During a year of use, this security system proved to be very helpful and easy to maintain.

Project length: September 1997–present

Name: **Rochester Hills Public Library Staff Intranet**
Library: Rochester Hills Public Library
Contact: Larry Neal, head of technical services
Address: Head of Technical Systems, Rochester Hills Public Library, Rochester, MI 48307-2043
Phone: (248) 650-7123; Fax: (248) 650-7121
E-mail: nealarry@metronet.lib.mi.us
Hardware: Hewlett Packard NetServer 5/133 LC, 4 GB hard drive, 64 MB RAM, Hewlett Packard SureStore 6000
Software: Microsoft Windows NT Server 4.0 service pack 3, Microsoft Internet Information Server 4.0, Microsoft Index Server 2.0, Microsoft FrontPage 98, Microsoft Office 97
Description: The purpose of Rochester Hills Public Library's Intranet was to create a ready reference resource for the entire staff without a significant amount of additional work. By modifying the way staff members save press releases, policies, and other documents, such files have become readily available for all staff. For example, rather than copying a press release and distributing it to all departments, a staff member can (with the appropriate permission) create a press release and save it on the Intranet. Although it is printed out as usual, a staff member can easily retrieve it from the Intranet using the search engine because the contents are fully indexed.

The Intranet also serves as a source for building procedures and training. Using color pictures and sound, a staff member can find everything needed to know about using voice mail as well as hear how each voice mail menu sounds. Step-by-step descriptions allow staff to quickly navigate through evacuation procedures using hyperlinks while not having to sort through the directions for all of the other departments.

To maintain staff interest in using the Intranet instead of traditional print sources for information, significant "personal" information has been added. A weekly message about current staff events is posted, and there is even a complete staff "yellow pages" with pictures of each staff member along with information about what the person does and some of his or her personal interests. The Intranet is just at the foundation stage, promising to finally bring a taste of the "paperless office" to RHPL. It has not been a revolution, rather the start of an evolution that continues to slowly expand on a monthly basis. It is a project that will never be "done," and planning for growth from the start has been key to keeping the project manageable.

Reference:	http://www.metronet.lib.mi.us/ROCH/intranet
Project length:	October 1997–present
Cost:	$3,000 for software, $250 for extra RAM, $380 for Microsoft Windows NT Server 4.0

Name:	**Starkville High School Library Automation Consortium**
Library:	Starkville High School Library
Contact:	Florence Box
Address:	603 Yellow Jacket Drive, Starkville, MS 39759
Phone:	(601) 324-4139
E-mail:	box@shs.starkville.k12.ms.us
Hardware:	IBM PC compatibles, printers, scanners, television studio equipment, copier, hubs
Software:	Library Automation System, Windows 95, Microsoft Word, Microsoft PowerPoint, and various CD-ROMs
Description:	Through a three-way cooperative effort, Starkville High School students have access not only to the high school's resources but also to those of two major universities. The school joined with Mississippi State and Mississippi University for Women to become the third member of the Golden Triangle Regional Library Consortium, sharing the Data Research Associates' circulation, patron, and online catalog programs. Playing an essential role in providing access is the local cable company, which allows use of cabling via fiber optic cable.

With finishing touches being completed, the 1,200 students at the high school have access to 75 computers in the library and 2 computer labs, all of which are networked and are Internet accessible. A television studio will be equipped in the near future for TV production courses.

Problems encountered were those typical of constructing and installing a network. The support of a consortium has been a great help. Increasing the number of library staff from the present two is being considered.

Project length: 1992–present
Cost: $29,000 per year; legislative funding is providing access to numerous databases

Management

Many management tasks can be enhanced with the aid of a microcomputer, including writing reports, preparing budgets, creating schedules, ordering materials, and doing accounting and payroll. Word processors, spreadsheets, and specialized payroll or accounting programs are useful in this regard. Just about any word processor will work when it comes to writing reports. WordPerfect, Microsoft Word, and others allow a librarian to create excellent looking monthly reports, newsletters, announcements, fliers, and posters. Another program, such as B&T Link from Baker and Taylor, is used to order books online, without mailing purchase orders. Confirmations are downloaded to the library immediately. The Mishawaka-Penn Public Library used a spreadsheet to calculate the best way to shift a journals collection. The University of Akron University Libraries uses a computer to track the use of electronic journals.

Name:	**Barcoding for Collection Analysis**
Library:	Northern Illinois University Libraries
Contact:	Elizabeth A. Titus, associate professor
Address:	136 FML, Northern Illinois University, De Kalb, IL 60115
Phone:	(815) 753-9701
E-mail:	etlives@niu.edu
Hardware:	Zenith 148, CGA monitor, 20 MB hard drive, EZ bar code system, Intermac 1545 scanner, 14-digit bar code labels, Reader Model PC (Timekeeping systems)
Software:	Alpha 4 version 2.1
Description:	The project systematically measures the use of in-house bound journal collections. Data is then used for space planning and collection development decisions. As bound journals are used and prior to their being reshelved, they are bar coded and scanned into a database that provides the library with incremental counts for each volume used. At the end of the year, reports on use pat-

terns of the bound volumes are available. This project is useful for those libraries that need data on how their bound periodicals are used either for collection development decisions or for those that are placing journals in remote storage.

Suggestions for developing this type of project include ensuring the integrity of the database and having only a few well-trained staff members do the data entry. It is important to integrate the process into the routine daily operations of the unit responsible for doing data entry. Critical to the success is the value the library administration places on data collection on use of journals, on systems staff and library operations staff working effectively in a team approach, and on all staff understanding how the collection use statistics provide critical information for collection development decision making.

Reference: Elizabeth Titus, W. Grant, and L. Haricombe, "Barcoding as a Tool for Collection Analysis," *Information Technology and Libraries* 13, no. 4 (1994): 257–65.
Project length: 1993–1995
Cost: Funded internally through the library operating budget

Name: **Library Activities Online Scheduling Project**
Library: Wichita State University Libraries
Contact: Gayle Gunderson, government information librarian
Address: Government Information Librarian, Wichita State University Library, Campus Box 68, Wichita, KS 67260-0068
Phone: (316) 978-5130; Fax: (316) 978-3048
E-mail: gunderso@twsuvm.uc.twsu.edu
Hardware: Intel 133 MHz PC with 64 MB RAM
Software: Linux 5.1, Synchronize 1.3.02r
Description: This online scheduling project is the implementation of a shared software program for librarywide and individual scheduling that is more accurate and more efficient, uses less paper, and is easier to use than a number of different paper calendars. The scheduling software allows scheduling for library staff schedules, reference desk staffing, a teaching room, library staff meeting rooms, and student study rooms.

Synchronize is a software program that serves as a scheduler, planner, calendar, and reminder for individuals, groups, and departments. The project began when one of the librarians obtained the software for the library on a trial basis, installed it on a Linux server, then installed the client software on the reference librarian's PCs running Windows 95, and encouraged people to give it a try. However, it became apparent that more prodding was needed to get people to really use Synchronize significantly. The reference and instruction team was able to get the approval of the reference librarians to let them use Synchronize to schedule the classroom for bibliographic instruction classes. It would serve as a good "test" and as a good example of what Synchronize could do. Using the new software for viewing and reserving the classroom proved to be a good way to introduce a new way of scheduling and to train people with Synchronize specifically. After the written reservations from the notebook were recorded into Synchronize, the scheduling book was removed completely since both systems cannot be in use simultaneously due to the risk of duplication or omission in the schedule for that room.

The new system has worked well. Since Synchronize is on everyone's computer, it eliminates many trips from offices to the notebook. This is a great help because the librarian can check immediately for room availability and make a reservation, eliminating the need to remember to make a follow-up telephone call to confirm the time. The schedule can then be printed out for those who still like it in print format. In addition, librarians and staff are encouraged to use the program as a personal scheduler to help them track their own projects.

It is apparent that this software can do a great deal more. It is planned to implement Synchronize for scheduling the reference desk and to apply it to other scheduling uses in the library.

Reference: http://www.crosswind.com
Project length: June 1998–present
Cost: $75 per user (in groups of 5) the first year and $15 per user for subsequent support and updates from the library's capital funds

Name: **Materials Ordering Using B&T Link**
Library: Maywood Public Library
Contact: Patrick R. Dewey, director
Address: 121 S. Fifth Ave., Maywood, IL 60153
Phone: (708) 343-1847; Fax: (708) 343-2115
E-mail: patrickdewey@hotmail.com
Hardware: Compaq Pentium PC, modem
Software: B&T Link
Description: B&T Link has significantly improved the library's ability to order and receive materials of all kinds through its primary vendor, Baker and Taylor. It was installed in about 15 minutes, and is

Management

simple to use. As book selections are collected from the library staff, orders are then placed into the system to create a book order. This order contains all necessary information to order the materials electronically from Baker and Taylor. Orders are checked against the system's database of 1.7 million titles. Most orders are placed into the system by ISBN. If this number is incorrect (if the ISBN does not match the title in the database), the system will sound an alert. If the ISBN is unknown, materials may be found by searching for them by title, author, etc. When found, the ISBN may be placed into the order directly from the search result screen. Once all items have been entered into the order, the order is saved. When ready to transmit, the computer will dial the number and upload the items. This takes just a minute or two. Once completed, the system returns a status report of all items including whether they are available, canceled, back-ordered, etc. Items begin arriving from the publisher within two days of the order. The software is very powerful and has a variety of features.

Project length: 1996–present

Name: **Monthly Report to the Library Board**
Library: Glenside Public Library District
Contact: Kathryn Vojtech
Address: 25 Fullerton Ave., Glendale Heights, IL 60139
Phone: (630) 260-1551; Fax: (630) 260-1433
Hardware: IBM PC compatible Pentium, inkjet printer
Software: Microsoft Word for Windows 95, Microsoft Excel
Description: The monthly report incorporates narrative and statistics from each department of the library including administration. Department managers submit their monthly reports to the team administrators (administrative librarian), and the team administrator edits the reports and gives them to the administrative assistant to create the monthly librarian's report. This same format is used each month. The previous month's document is saved on disk and hard drive and updated by the administrative assistant. The monthly librarian's report is distributed to library trustees in their board meeting packets and is posted for staff. This process is expected to be revised once the staff LAN is complete. The statistical portion of the report makes comparisons with the prior year on the measures of circulation, new materials added, number of volumes, new library cards issued, meeting room book-

ings, computer bookings, reference transactions, and attendance at programs.
Project length: 1983–present
Cost: Funding from the operating budget; total costs not known

Name: **Payroll Using an Online Service**
Library: Maywood Public Library
Contact: Patrick R. Dewey, director
Address: 121 S. Fifth Ave., Maywood, IL 60153
Phone: (708) 343-1847; Fax (708) 343-2115
E-mail: patrickdewey@hotmail.com
Hardware: IBM PC 486, Hewlett Packard LaserJet 4 Plus
Software: Safe-Pay Connection
Description: Using Safe-Pay Connection, the library automated the transmission of payroll information to the company that provides reports and paychecks. Once up and operating, this project has gone smoothly. Once every two weeks, the business office staff uploads the payroll information to the payroll company. The next day the paychecks are delivered to the library.

The few problems are nearly all due to faults such as in telephone lines rather than to the software or upload process. There is nothing difficult or special about the installation or setup routines. This DOS-based program has few menus or options. The installation program allows for twelve different types of businesses from which to choose. It comes with a tutorial on how to enter data and send the payroll information electronically.

After employee data has been entered, it may be retrieved by employee ID, name, or social security number. The main menu allows access to employee maintenance, off-line checks, payroll entry, transfer files, company maintenance, utilities, clear files, or end. At Maywood, the usual routine involves entering employee payroll data through the payroll entry option and then transferring files by modem.

The software also comes with a manual that has complete details and descriptions and some screen shots. The employee maintenance option allows the system to add or edit employee records and list changes. It also contains some employee file utilities. The payroll entry menu allows the user to create payroll worksheets, enter earnings (hours entry), determine pay totals, and produce pay reports.
Project length: 1996–present

Management **85**

Name:	**Training-Center Schedule**
Library:	Ann Arbor District Library
Contact:	Colleen Verge
Address:	343 S. Fifth Ave., Ann Arbor, MI 48104
Phone:	(743) 327-8331
E-mail:	vergec@aadl.org
Hardware:	Dell Pentium connected to the library's wide area network
Software:	Microsoft Excel
Description:	The purpose of this project was to streamline scheduling and to track statistics of public classes. The Ann Arbor District Library offers regular classes that teach the public use of the library's electronic resources, the Internet, and other computer basics. A brochure schedule of the classes is published quarterly. Since the library has four separate locations, it needs to schedule the classes with limited conflict between branch locations to avoid their competing with each other.

Each quarter Microsoft Excel is used initially to create a file that is a master schedule of classes without dates and times. This file is placed on the wide area network in a directory that each location can access. Each location has one month to update this spreadsheet with the dates and times they will be offering classes. The spreadsheet is used to sort by date to check on schedule conflicts or by branch location to print out a separate list for each branch. A spreadsheet is also used to allocate substitute hours for those librarians who teach classes.

After each class is complete, statistics on the number of attendees are recorded on this same spreadsheet. A separate spreadsheet keeps track of where the public heard about the classes.

It is important to make sure each staff member who needs access to this spreadsheet has permission to access it by the system administrator. Since so many people have access to this spreadsheet it occasionally gets corrupted. Therefore, once the statistics have been added to this sheet, it is protected with a password. It is also necessary to back up files.

Project length:	1997–present
Cost:	None

Name:	**Using a Spreadsheet to Shift a Journal Collection**
Library:	Mishawaka-Penn Public Library
Contact:	Dennis C. Tucker
Address:	6202 Morenci Tr., Indianapolis, IN 46268
Phone:	(317) 298-6570

E-mail:	Dennis@palni.edu
Hardware:	IBM PC compatible
Software:	Lotus 1-2-3 (or any spreadsheet software)
Description:	Due to the growth in the library's collection of bound and boxed serials, it became necessary to shift a number of runs of titles to storage. The effort involved shifting journals in both the on-site and remote storage areas. Rather than shift the collection by trial and error, using physical labor, it was decided to plan the shift electronically, using an electronic spreadsheet.

Exact measurements were taken for the existing length for each title (in linear inches) and the amount of annual growth for each title. The resulting data was entered into a spreadsheet, and formulas were applied to calculate growth and necessary shelf space. Thus, titles were shifted often in electronic format but only once in reality, saving staff time and effort.

References:	Dennis C. Tucker, "Using a Spreadsheet Program to Shift a Journal Collection," *College & Research Libraries News* 10 (Nov. 1989): 904–9.
	Dennis C. Tucker, *Library Relocations and Collection Shifts* (Medford, N.J.: Information Today, 1999).
Project length:	1989
Cost:	Staff time; software and hardware were already owned

Name:	**Vitreous Proxy Server**
Library:	Science and Technology Library, The University of Akron University Libraries
Contact:	Aimee deChambeau, University Libraries; Dr. Abdullah Abonamah, Mathematics and Computer Science Department
Address:	ASEC 104, The University of Akron, Akron, OH 44325-3907
Phone:	(330) 972-6262
E-mail:	daimee@uakron.edu
Hardware:	Server, 2 workstations, 16-port RJ-45 Ethernet hub, 8 GB internal tape drive, Windows NT 4.0 server and workstation
Software:	C++, JAVA
Description:	Journal use studies have long been conducted by libraries to determine which titles to keep and which to cancel, discard, or send to remote storage. These traditional use studies, however, are beginning to fall short due to the increasing use of computers for storage of and access to journals. The vitreous proxy server scheme was designed specifically to collect electronic-journal use statistics and produce a set of management reports on their usage.

These management reports include access counts broken down by site, specific location origin/domain, and specific journal issue. The reports also graphically display site analysis reports, showing usage of electronic journals on a daily, weekly, monthly, and annual basis. Using this information, the University Libraries can make appropriate decisions regarding these services.

The vitreous proxy server project is implemented using JAVA, thereby ensuring security and robustness. User confidentiality is maintained at all times by restricting the server to examine only IP packets that are destined to an electronic journal site, and by parsing only the initial request to that site.

The project is coordinated and carried out by a faculty member from the Department of Mathematics and Computer Science and one from the University Libraries. Graduate students assist in the implementation of hardware and software solutions. University Libraries' faculty and staff assist in the creation of tailored reports generated by the server, and the University Libraries' Administration receives all reports to distribute for use in the evaluation of electronic journal services.

Project length: July 1998–summer of 1999
Cost: Approximately $10,000

Periodicals

Locating and ordering periodicals is a time-consuming and often slow endeavor. The libraries in this section have gone to great lengths to make the material more available and timely in its use. Unicom Corporate Library routes magazines in electronic format to save time. The J. Y. Joyner Library has created the North Carolina Periodicals Index that indexes forty-five valuable but unindexed periodicals for local use using the Microsoft Excel database.

Name:	**Electronic Magazine Routing**
Library:	Unicom Corporate Library
Contact:	Bobbie Goering
Address:	227 West Monroe, Chicago, IL 60606
Phone:	(312) 394-3064
E-mail:	roberta.j.goering@ucm.com
Hardware:	Local area network, wide area network, IBM PCs
Software:	E-mail, Microsoft Outlook
Description:	The library used to order multiple copies of key utility periodicals and route or share them with readers at stations and offices all over Northern Illinois. Unique publications in this industry can be $1,000 or more per year. Unfortunately, sharing magazines takes time. It is common for the last person on a routing list to see a magazine or newsletter six months after publication date. Except for those who were first on a routing list, all of the library's customers were chronically unhappy. E-mail and Microsoft Outlook have improved this situation.

Key suppliers now send publications electronically, and Outlook stores these publications in public folders. One folder is set up for each title. As new editions arrive, the library staff moves the publication from e-mail to the appropriate folder. (Moving is by click and drag.) With Microsoft Outlook, viewing is limited to those on an access list, therefore complying with license requirements. As added value, a reminder is sent to all on the access list when a new edition arrives. People don't have to remember to check the public folders, and this affords an opportunity to gently remind readers of copyright restrictions. Everyone on the access list can read a periodical on the date it is delivered to the library.

Project length: Ongoing
Cost: None

Name: **North Carolina Periodicals Index**
Library: J. Y. Joyner Library, East Carolina University
Contact: Maurice C. York
Address: J. Y. Joyner Library, East Carolina University, Greenville, NC 27858
Phone: (252) 328-0252
E-mail: yorkm@mail.ecu.edu
Hardware: IBM PCs
Software: Microsoft Excel, Microsoft Word
Description: The periodicals index project was undertaken to provide greater access to forty-five valuable but unindexed periodicals owned by the library. Articles and reviews less than one page were generally not entered into the index unless they were judged to be especially useful to students.

Working with public service departments from around North Carolina, the systems department designed a database using Microsoft Excel. Included in the index were fields for full bibliographic data, an abstract, notes, and up to four separate Library of Congress subject headings. To avoid repeat typing, drop-down lists were created for periodical titles, title abbreviations, and months. A thesaurus was also included of previously used subject headings to avoid retyping. To collect data, a paper form is used that includes the fields in the Excel database. Members of the staff work with the paper form to index journals, then the information is sent to the systems department to be input into the database. It is updated with new entries every two months. To do this, the systems department must convert the data using the mail merge feature of a word processing program. Once it has been completed, it is turned into a text file. Microsoft Word is used (find/replace) to remove all blank or unused fields from the database. The completed file is then appended to the database on the library's UNIX-based Web server. The final step involves reindexing the whole file with the WAIS-sf software program available free over the Internet.

Users of the index find an explanation of how to use the index and can search it by keyword or by Boolean commands, truncation, and even literal phrases. Anyone can use the index since it is available on the Internet without a password. The results have been outstanding. Students are using these periodicals much more heavily than they were without an index. They also find it very easy to use.

Reference: Maurice C. York, "Value-Added Reference Service: The North Carolina Periodicals Index," *Computers in Libraries* (May 1997): 30. Available at http://fringe.lib.ecu.edu

Project length: 1992–present

Public Access and Student and Patron Training

Comparison of today's opportunities to serve the public and to provide information with the world as it was just fifteen years ago is enough to inspire awe in any librarian. Public access to microcomputers in a library setting goes back just about to the time that microcomputers were invented; the practice has become increasingly popular ever since. Public microcomputers are used for reference, for access to the Internet, and to access applications software. Some libraries that have the available resources provide workshops and classes on the use of hardware and individual software packages.

Computers for the public are usually stand-alone workstations designed for a specific purpose; sometimes, however, they are congregated into a lab setting, often joined as a local area network. A lab full of computers must have its own set of rules. For more information, read the projects in the chapter on computer labs in this book.

For several reasons, software selection for public access is much easier than it used to be. First, there is now a very large selection of high quality software to choose from at reasonable prices. In addition, many good educational software catalogs exist that include suitable programs for all age groups. Software can be purchased as large collections of shareware. The single caveat regards licensing: some software can be used only by the original owner.

Circulating software to patrons' homes is a much better and easier operation than it used to be because most software is available on CD-ROM and is close to being indestructible.

Although the problems associated with all of these new services are many, they may be divided into the areas of security of hardware and software; staffing for assistance, training, and oversight; and hardware and software selection and installation. The Internet has provided some additional problems to think about, primarily in the form of filtering problems that may necessitate a written public policy regarding the use of the Internet in the library.

The projects in this chapter provide some understanding of how many libraries have gone about providing and using the new electronic services, the types of problems they have encountered, and what successes they have had.

An excellent example of the history and development of public access has taken place at the Chicago Public Library. It began with one Apple II computer in 1980 that quickly became popular beyond belief. Now the Chicago Public Library has dozens of PCs available at branch libraries and an entire lab full at the Harold Washington Library Center downtown. A popular lab for the public has been active at the Portage-Cragin branch of the Chicago Public Library. Three of these projects are included.

Other projects in this chapter include the creation of an Internet tutorial on legal research by the University of North Carolina Law Library, the digitization of a collection for twenty-four-hour Web access by Michigan State University, and the Martin Memorial Library, which hosts a regular meeting of the White Rose Computer Club.

Name:	**Bibliographic Instruction**
Library:	University of North Carolina Law Library
Contact:	Robert C. Vreeland, reference/electronic services librarian
Address:	CB #3385, Chapel Hill, NC 27599
Phone:	(919) 962-2561
E-mail:	vreeland@email.unc.edu
Hardware:	Dell PowerEdge server running Linux, digital camera, flatbed scanner
Software:	Freeware Perl scripts, JavaScript, Xcmacs, Adobe Acrobat, Adobe Pagemill, Adobe Premiere, Corel Draw 8, Ricoh Photostudio
Description:	An Internet tutorial was needed to provide an introduction to the fundamentals of legal research. Library staff provide bibliographic instruction to hundreds of students per year. The purpose of this project was to create an alternative means to learn how to use the law library. The solution was to put a tutorial online using the Internet.
	It is important to plan the uses of the project. Is it to be a substitute for traditional bibliographic instruction? A supplement to it? A completely separate means of communicating with users? The decision will determine how extensive the tutorial's discussion needs to be.
	Finding personnel to work on a project of this nature can be difficult, since it requires both technical expertise and familiarity with the academic discipline involved. Content and design issues will tend to be intertwined due to the pedagogic nature of the project. The professors who typically bring students to the library instruction should be made aware of its availability so

that they encourage, or even require, students to view the material online.

To improve the project, feedback should be collected from a form on the Web site or from paper surveys distributed to classes. Some mechanism should be available for students to determine exactly how much of the material they understand. One means of achieving this is to include an online multiple-choice test at the end of the tutorial. This can provide an instant assessment for the user, an opportunity to ask a librarian for assistance, or an alert that the student should read through the tutorial again.

Reference:	http://library.law.unc.edu/tutorial
Project length:	Ongoing
Cost:	$2,705 UNC 1997–98 Chancellor's Instructional Technology Grant; plus developer's labor costs

Name:	**Computer Literacy: A Multilingual Approach**
Library:	Portage-Cragin Branch Library Computer Center, Chicago Public Library
Contact:	Kevin Latham
Address:	5108 W. Belmont Ave., Chicago, IL 60641
Phone:	(312) 744-2820
E-mail:	klatham@hotmail.com
Hardware:	Compaq Pentium DeskPro 590 computers, 2 Compaq Pentium DeskPro 5120 computers, 2 Hewlett Packard LaserJet printers, 1 Lexmark Optra R+ printer
Software:	English-, Polish-, and Spanish-language versions of Microsoft Windows 3.1, Microsoft Word 6.0 for Windows, and Microsoft Works 3.0 for Windows; Accent Professional for Windows (multilingual word processor)
Description:	The project began with a grant to allow bilingual and foreign-language patrons equal access to services within the computer center. It expanded services to the Polish and Spanish communities by providing the latest technology in computers, software in Polish and Spanish, help (tutorial programs and a full-time staff of two instructors) for beginners, and a book collection in Polish and Spanish to support the computers and software.

One computer was designated as the Polish-language computer and another as the Spanish-language computer. Foreign-speaking patrons were offered assistance by bilingual staff members.

To succeed with a project such as this, staff should be sure there are enough computers available to dedicate one or more to a foreign language. If not, both English and foreign-language versions of the software may be installed on a single computer. (Use different directory names: for example, install the English version of Windows 3.1 in a directory named c:\windows and the Polish version of Windows 3.1 in a directory named c:\polish.)

It can be difficult to make sure that bilingual staff members will always be available when needed. Therefore, it is necessary to have patrons schedule appointments. It is especially rewarding to bilingual staff to become involved in such a project because they assist members of their own community. Without bilingual staff it is not possible to provide patrons with the needed assistance.

Project length: July 1995–present
Cost: $20,000 from federal LSCA funding administered by the Illinois State Library

Name: **Digital Images from the American Radicalism Collection**
Library: Michigan State University Libraries
Contact: Michael Seadle, editor, *Library Hi Tech*
Address: 100 Library, Michigan State University, East Lansing, MI 48824-1048
Phone: (517) 432-0807
E-mail: seadle@mail.lib.msu.edu
Hardware: Minolta PS-3000 overhead scanner, 2 Pentium PCs
Software: Epic, Rexx, Hijack Pro 2.0, Netscape Navigator
Description: This project's goal was to support the curriculum of special sections of the American Thought and Language course, an introductory writing class. For years students from the American Thought and Language classes have come to MSU Libraries' special collections department to get materials to write papers on American radicalism. Since special collections had limited hours, and since the extra handling was hard on some materials, it was decided to scan a sampling of them and make them available on the Web. Because of concerns for students working with slow modems, the images were made as small as possible without losing legibility. The interface was made as simple as possible so that no one had to learn how to download extra software.

Bibliographic instruction was an important part of this project. Each class that used these materials first attended a session in which they were shown how to access the Web site, how to use the subject list, and how to navigate from page to page through individual documents.

Student feedback from the project was overwhelmingly positive, despite some problems printing the images. Because these materials are freely available on the Web, many other students have used them too, both within MSU and from around the world.

Slowly the documents are being keyed in and made available in SGML (Standard Generalized Markup Language) as well as in image form. Keying the documents will allow students to search them, and SGML markup will enable search engines to use structural elements so that, for example, a word or phrase could be searched just in the chapter headings (instead of everywhere in the text). Keying text is a slower and more expensive process that also requires careful proofreading. It could be years before all the images have matching SGML text.

References: Michael Seadle, "Building on the Cornell-Yale Model: Digitizing the Radicalism Collection at Michigan State University," *Library Hi Tech* 16, no. 2 (1998): 19–36.

"Digitization for the Masses," *Reference Services Review* 25, no. 4 (fall/winter 1997): 119.

Project length: June 1997–June 1998
Cost: Approximately $5,400 in student labor

Name: **Introduction to Computers and the Internet**
Library: Essex Branch, Baltimore County Public Library
Contact: Kathy Slader
Address: 1110 Eastern Blvd., Baltimore, MD 21221
Phone: (410) 887-0295
E-mail: ksladek@bcpl.net
Hardware: Gateway 2000 PC, projection screen
Software: Microsoft Internet Explorer, Eudora Pro E-Mail, Microsoft PowerPoint, Microsoft Word, Microsoft Excel
Description: This program series was designed to introduce the public to current computer trends. The Essex Branch was one of the original nine library branches in the county to benefit from the Microsoft/ALA libraries online project. The community's need for basic instruction on computer and Internet principles soon became evident. The library was presenting regular demonstrations on how to use the Internet, but the scope of the questions was soon exceeding them. The project onsite administrator designed a series of demonstration programs to suit these needs. She created PowerPoint presentations on e-mail and basic home-page design and made handouts using Microsoft Word and Microsoft

Excel. She created a Web page for an introduction to computers.

The demonstrations are very popular. The only complaint has been the lack of hands-on time.

The series includes intro to computers, intro to the Internet, intro to e-mail, and intro to the home page. The presentations are still being updated and are given approximately three times per year, each two hours once a week for a total of four weeks.

Project length: Ongoing

Name: **Literacy Links: Adult Literacy/ESL Services**
Library: Arlington Heights Memorial Library
Contact: Gaylia Grant, adult literacy/ESL services specialist
Address: 500 N. Dunton Ave., Arlington Heights, IL 60004
Phone: (847) 506-2632
E-mail: ggrant@nslsilus.org
Hardware: Dell Dimension multimedia computers XPS 200 MHz, Ultrascan color monitors 1000TX and D1025HTX, Panasonic CD-ROM changers, speakers, microphones, headphones
Software: Ellis Intro, Middle Mastery, Master Pronunciation, Descriptive 2010, Learning 2000 Lifetime Library, Focus on Grammar, English Vocabulary, Career English, Mavis Beacon Teaches Typing
Description: To provide computer-assisted help to those needing adult literacy skills and to facilitate language acquisition of adult English as a Second Language (ESL), four computers were set up in carrels. Therefore, students could work on their literacy skills on interactive, multimedia software without being disturbed by others. The study carrels were placed against one wall of the literacy office.

Each computer is equipped with word processing. Access to the Internet is planned. Available software includes hundreds of hours of instructions for students on all levels. Students may work at their own pace, advancing when ready, and monitoring themselves.

One significant problem was the amount of time it took to install and configure the software programs because the technology staff was already overburdened. Therefore, hiring an outside consultant or assistant to do the setup might be advisable.

Project length: November 1997–present
Cost: $20,265 from an LSCA grant through the Illinois State Library

Name:	**Meeting Training Demands through Videoconferencing**
Library:	Rochester Regional Library Council
Contact:	Kathleen M. Miller
Address:	390 Packett's Landing, P.O. Box 66160, Fairport, NY 14450
Phone:	(716) 223-7570
Hardware:	Intel P5-200 with MMX technology desktop computer, 64 MB RAM, 17″ monitor; Intel ProShare Video System 200; Canon VC-C11 MKII video camera with motorized pan-tilt-zoom, wireless remote, six presets, optional wide-angle lens adapter, 450 TV lines resolution; PolyCom SoundStation EX, full-duplex with 360 degree pick-up, two extended microphones, optional wireless microphone; IBID PC White board; 29″ SVGA monitor; 128 Kbps ISDN lines; instructor workstation and monitor stand for each site
Software:	Full-duplex video and audio conferencing software; Microsoft Windows 95, Microsoft Windows 98, Microsoft Access, Netscape Navigator, Microsoft Internet Explorer, Microsoft Office 95 Professional, Netscape Communicator
Description:	Using a combination of computer and video equipment, the Rochester Regional Library Council set up a training program in the council's headquarters building for hands-on instruction for computer skills required for electronic doorway library skills for library personnel and council-sponsored programs. There is an instructor's workstation plus eight student workstations that accommodate two students each. Online at the council's Web site are the guidelines for use.
Reference:	http://www.rrlc.org/rrlctc.html
Project length:	January–June 1997
Cost:	$20,180

Name:	**Online Bibliographic Instruction for Research and Library Use**
Library:	Emmanuel College Library
Contact:	Dr. Mary Ann Tricarico, director
Address:	400 The Fenway, Boston, MA 02115
Phone:	(617) 264-7656
E-mail:	tricaric@emmanuel.edu
Hardware:	IBM PC Pentium
Software:	Authorware
Description:	A set of shared electronic tools provides online bibliographic instruction for the five colleges of The Fenway. Emmanuel College Library directed a project to design online bibliographic

instruction tutorials for use at the libraries. The staff wrote the text for a tutorial that is a self-paced, self-directed online guide for students to develop basic library research skills and information seeking skills. A consultant developed the online module from the text and then trained the staff to use Authorware software to design additional modules. The first module was completed in August 1998 and is used in general library orientation programs for new students, bibliographic instruction classes, and self-instruction. The project was evaluated at the end of the fall 1998 semester and additional modules are being designed for more-advanced research skills.

Project length: Development June–September 1998; ongoing
Cost: $12,122 from a Davis Foundation Educational Grant

Name: **Patron Training and Empowerment**
Library: Niles Public Library District
Contact: Sophia Anastos
Address: 6960 Oakton St., Niles, IL 60714
Phone: (847) 663-6636
E-mail: Sophia@nslsilus.org
Hardware: Pentium 150 or above, 32 MB memory or above, headphones
Software: ViaGrafix training videos
Description: Occasionally, people walk into the computer lab and say, "I don't know anything about computers, but I want to learn. Where do I start?" or, "I don't know how to use computers, but I have a job interview and need to type a résumé" or, "How do I use the Internet?" The library slowly accumulated training materials (mostly CD-ROMs) that started with the basics, like Microsoft Word, and the collection increased from there. The tutorials do not require that the application be installed. For example, even though the systems have been upgraded to Microsoft Word 97, tutorials can be run on previously released versions of Microsoft Word. Patrons come in at their level of expertise, which varies from "I'd like to be more proficient in C++ programming," to "How do I use a mouse?" They are given the CD-ROM that they need and a set of headphones, and they're on their way.

A number of patrons have upgraded their skills, qualified for better jobs, gotten over being afraid of computers, and added the Internet to their repertoire of available resources as a result. Library staff are happy to be a resource in these emerging technologies. No longer are patrons at the mercy of manuals, nor do the staff have to babysit them through the basics with little hope

Project length:	February 1997–present
Cost:	$400 to $1,000 for videotapes

Name:	**Pilot Computer Training Center**
Library:	David S. Kitson Memorial Library
Contact:	J. Howell
Address:	David S. Kitson Foundation, AJO 1067, P.O. Box 025216, Miami, FL 33102-5216
E-mail:	jhowell@ix.netcom.com
Hardware:	2 PCs
Software:	Word processing, database management
Description:	The David S. Kitson Memorial Library is a nonprofit association incorporated under the laws of Costa Rica. This project was initiated in memory of David S. Kitson, a local activist. The library maintains a pilot computer training center for young people. The problems associated with this project are many, including not enough computers. The library relies on donations of old 386 and 486 computer hardware to provide the equipment. Programs on the computers provide elementary instruction on the use of database management systems, word processing, and spreadsheets. Students also get the opportunity to learn the basics of computer literacy: how to turn the computer on, install programs, use the mouse, use Windows, etc. High school students use the computers to develop computer-related job skills. Though the computers are owned, maintained, and used by the library, they are housed, at least temporarily, in a local grade school. Since so many of the library's patrons speak Spanish, a challenge has been to obtain computer manuals in Spanish. The library actively seeks donations.
Reference:	http://www.discoverypress.com/lib-com.html
Project length:	Ongoing

Name:	**Public Access Microcomputers at the Chicago Public Library**
Library:	The Chicago Public Library
Address:	Harold Washington Library Center, 400 S. State St., Chicago, IL 60605
Hardware:	IBM PC compatibles and Macintosh
Software:	Word processing, spreadsheets, children's educational programs, Microsoft Publisher, Microsoft Word, Microsoft Access,

Microsoft Excel, Microsoft Works, Microsoft Office, Microsoft PowerPoint, Mavis Beacon Teaches Typing, WordPerfect, Adobe PageMaker

Description: The Chicago Public Library is a library system that serves the millions of residents of the City of Chicago and provides reciprocal borrowing and services to surrounding communities and to the State of Illinois.

The library's set of "Guidelines for Chicago Public Library Computer Use" is available online at www.chipublib.org/003cpl/computer/guidelines.html. Use of computers is on a first-come, first-served basis, and children under the age of seven must be accompanied by an adult. Appointments are for 30 minutes and are held for 10 minutes only. Some computers can be booked ahead up to one week. Reservations may be made by phone. Some locations that have advanced uses, such as word processing and spreadsheets, allow appointments for up to two hours. The guidelines state that no one is allowed to install or use any equipment or software not installed by the Chicago Public Library. In addition, no personal files may be saved to a hard drive. While Internet use is allowed, relay chats, newsgroups, and e-mail services are not. Laptop computers may be used in the library but only at the user's risk. Cords may not be plugged in so as to interfere with walkways, etc. For patron convenience, formatted disks may be purchased for $2 each.

The Computer Connection at the Harold Washington Library Center is the equivalent of a large public lab. It includes 22 IBM PCs and 5 Macintosh computers. Software includes Microsoft Works and Microsoft Office 95, including Access 7.0 for databases, Excel 7.0 for spreadsheets, PowerPoint 7.0 for presentations, Word 7.0 for word processing, and Publisher 7.0 for desktop publishing. WordPerfect 6.0 and Mavis Beacon Teaches Typing are also available on the IBM PCs. Macintosh applications include Adobe PageMaker 5.0, Microsoft Word 6.0, Microsoft Excel 5.0, mouse practice, and Mavis Beacon Typing Tutor. Laser printing is also available. The Computer Connection also has four PCs equipped for Internet use with Netscape.

The Computer Connection has an interesting way to handle patron files. The computers are networked and do not have "A" drives. Programs are sent from the server to the workstation for use. If patrons wish to save their work, they save it to the "E" drive. They must then go to the desk where staff will transfer it to their floppy diskette.

Reference: www.chipublib.org
Project length: Ongoing

Name: **Public Computer Use for Word Processing and the Internet**
Library: Russell Library
Contact: Catherine Ahern
Address: 123 Broad St., Middletown, CT 06457
Phone: (860) 344-8479
Hardware: 4 PCs, 4 Macintosh computers
Software: Microsoft Word, ClarisWorks, WordPerfect 5.1, and Type!
Description: The Russell Library has shown that it is important to keep pace with patron needs. Since 1990, the library has steadily added computer hardware, software, and services to increase access to the world of information. It has also adapted its physical structure to accommodate PCs for the public. Funding has been received through special grants. The staff envisions the creation of a computer center that will make possible classes for young people and adults. The first service offered in 1990 was word processing. There is no charge for computer use except for paper used in the printing of résumés, reports, and other documents.

The advent of the Internet brought demand for access to it as well. The library started to offer access to the Web with two PCs in the adult section and one in the children's room. Eventually, a third station was added on the adult side for any Web use. However, first priority was given to job seekers because a Labor Department grant purchased the station. The library has obtained funds to turn the current administrative area into a computer center, where all word processors and Internet computers for adults and children will go.

Project length: 1990–present
Cost: $2,000 startup costs; $1,000–$2,000 per year annual costs

Name: **Public Computer Workstations**
Library: Lewis J. Ort Library, Frostburg State University
Contact: Randall A. Lowe
Address: 1 Stadium Dr., Frostburg, MD 21532
Phone: (301) 687-4313
E-mail: d21blowe@frs00.fsu.umd.edu
Hardware: 16 Gateway 2000 Pentium and Pentium IIs with 32 and 64 MB RAM, 2 Hewlett Packard 4000 printers
Software: WinU, WinSelect, McAfee VirusScan, Netscape Navigator, Windows 95

Description: During the 1997–1998 academic year, the Lewis J. Ort Library of Frostburg State University (FSU), along with other libraries in the university system of Maryland, began the process of subscribing to and accessing article and other research databases through the World Wide Web. At the beginning of the academic year, the library had only one Internet personal computer available for public use. The computers needed to serve as an electronic kiosk, which would require menuing software and a method of securing each machine. Without a server, each PC, including all software installed, would need to be maintained separately. There was not enough staff to adequately run a large number of computers with this much software. Therefore, it was decided to follow a "middle road" until the server could be purchased. After a couple of months of research and intense testing of various software packages, it was decided that third-party menu and security software would be most effective and that only about 6 to 10 computers would be made available. (This was eventually expanded to 16.)

A large hard drive is not required if the PCs are only going to be used as kiosks. The combination of software was easy to install and maintain, and it met the criteria of a secure electronic kiosk for users. Any library, especially a small one, that has the required wiring in its building for Internet access would find this setup easy to install and maintain.

WinU replaces the Windows computer desktop with a menu that is organized by subject to allow access to the library's Web-based databases. It also provides various levels of security. It prevents users from accessing the "my computer" or "start buttons" of Windows 95. It also locks CD-ROM drives on the PC. It provides for running applications maximized and for running them one at a time. Statistics are kept on the number of times menu options are chosen. Web site and printing usage are also tracked. Finally, WinU allows menus to be created at one PC; clones of these menus can be copied onto a floppy disk and then quickly copied to public PCs.

WinSelect allows Internet downloading to be restricted to the floppy drive of the computer. It is also used to disable Windows "hotkeys," so users cannot access the operating system. It also disables right-side mouse clicks. WinSelect may be used to stop certain types of applications from being executed or certain files from being altered. WinSelect can be set to limit the number of pages that may be printed. This software is easy to install, and once set up, there is no need to touch it again.

Frostburg State University has a site license for McAfee VirusScan, which allows users' floppy disks to be scanned as well as the computer's fixed disks. It also enables an FTP site to be checked for updates, so the system can always check for the latest virus.

FSU uses Netscape Navigator as its browser. The library staff did not want users to create large bookmark files or make permanent changes to local preference settings (such as the home page setting). Locating the Netscape bookmark.htm and prefs.ds files on the computer and setting them to "read only" easily solves these problems. In Windows 95, this is done by highlighting the file and changing its properties to read only. Windows 95 networking is used to network PCs to two Hewlett Packard 4000 printers.

This configuration has worked well. However, the number of PCs that can be realistically maintained is limited due to the amount of time it takes to make changes to the menus and make other software updates. Initially, it takes approximately 30 minutes to set up a PC. To make changes to software or menu updates, the security on each PC must be disabled, which requires changing settings and rebooting. The process can be time consuming. A final problem that may occur with the above configuration is the response of both the operating system and the various software packages to running simultaneously. With one McAfee update, the new software did not work well with WinU or WinSelect, resulting in a Windows 95 crash. There is also occasional freezing up of computers. However, these problems have not recurred with any other software updates. If menus or other configurations are not going to be changed very often, the programs will require little maintenance after initial installation.

Project length:	Fall 1997–present
Cost:	$1,200; $25 per machine for WinSelect; $350 for 10 computers for McAfee VirusScan

Name:	**Résumé Workshop at the Computer Center**
Library:	Portage-Cragin Branch Computer Center, Chicago Public Library
Contact:	Kevin Latham
Address:	5108 W. Belmont Ave., Chicago, IL 60641

Phone:	(312) 744-2820
E-mail:	klatham@hotmail.com
Hardware:	3 Compaq Pentium DeskPro 590 computers, 2 Hewlett Packard LaserJet printers, 1 Lexmark Optra R+ printer
Software:	Microsoft Word 6.0 for Windows, WordPerfect 6.1 for Windows, and WordPerfect 7.0 for Windows 95
Description:	The goal of this project was to help library patrons create a high quality résumé and cover letter as quickly and easily as possible. Patrons who have never created a résumé before are given a résumé form that helps them gather the information necessary to create a résumé. After completing the form, they make an appointment to type the résumé. Patrons choose a template from among the fifteen different layouts available. Indent markers instead of the tabs are used to create a layout, thus making it less likely that a patron will disturb the layout of the résumé. Patrons type over the templates on an IBM or compatible in typeover mode. A staff member assists them if necessary. Upon completion, a librarian helps proofread and revise the résumé. Patrons may then print free copies on résumé paper or on the library's paper. Résumés are saved on the patrons' disks or stored on a special résumé disk kept at the branch. Recently, a patron donated several hundred used disks that are now given to patrons who do not have a disk.

It is necessary to find a variety of templates that are both pleasing to the eye and easy for a patron to type over. The biggest problem encountered were patrons who were under the impression that library staff would compose and type the résumé for them. Patrons are now informed at the beginning that they must do their share of the work. Another problem is in printing final copies. A résumé should be revised thoroughly before printing multiple copies. Patrons are limited to ten copies, so they won't print too many copies in the event of an error.

Assisting patrons in résumé production is difficult and requires patience. Staff members need the necessary combination of computer and writing skills. It is best to have a professional revise the résumés. |
| Project length: | March 1992–present |
| Cost: | No cost; completed by library staff, on library time, and with library equipment and supplies |

Name:	**White Rose IBM Computer Enthusiasts Library Club**
Library:	Martin Memorial Library
Description:	This computer club meets at the Martin Memorial Library twice each month. Membership dues are $25 per year per family. A full-time individual student membership is $10 per year. Benefits include access to the club's BBS that contains freeware, shareware, and public domain software, available at 14,000 bps. The goal of the club is to encourage all efforts and activities in connection with the IBM or compatible home computer, promote a full discussion and exchange of ideas regarding the planning and conduct of such activities, disseminate the significant results of all these efforts and activities, and promote a better understanding and appreciation of the versatility and usefulness of the IBM or compatible home computer. Membership is open to anyone interested in the purpose and objectives of this users group.
	The club is divided into special interest groups. Continuing discussion includes the latest software, hardware, gadgets, and computer news. The club is an excellent way for users to exchange information, suggestions, and advice regarding all aspects of microcomputer hardware and software. It is a not-for-profit organization. Meetings include a question and answer session and demonstrations of products. The club has the use of the library's computer center. A newsletter is sent out regularly to members. Local and major computer hardware and software vendors are also invited to show products. Occasionally, members receive group discounts.
Project length:	1980–present
Cost:	None

Public Relations

A microcomputer can improve a library's public relations effort in many ways. Two examples are included here. The Park Ridge Public Library used its microcomputer to generate cable television programming for public relations. The TV channel beams exciting informational screens to subscribers' homes 24 hours each day. The library has a free cable guide that is available in the reader's services department. Portsmouth Public Library patrons used a microcomputer to create a slide show to celebrate the 375th anniversary of the community.

Name:	**The Library Cable Network: Public Relations through Cable Television**
Library:	Park Ridge Public Library
Contact:	Larry Kleckner
Address:	20 S. Prospect Ave., Park Ridge, IL 60068
Phone:	(847) 825-3123 x202
E-mail:	lkleckner@park-ridge.lib.il.us
Hardware:	Windows NT network with Pentium staff computers, digital camera, scanner, video card with composite video output, multiple disk CD player for continuous playback of noncopyrighted music
Software:	Microsoft PowerPoint
Description:	The Park Ridge Public Library creates information screens for local public access cable TV using a microcomputer and PowerPoint presentation software. This is a unique vehicle for delivering library information to the community. In addition to the usual newsletters, fliers, home pages, and posters that describe the library's activities, the screens bring the information into community homes and businesses through their television cable network. The screens attractively present information about programs, services, hours, collections, and checkout information. Also, advertisements and information for most library programs are included. Each screen takes approximately one-half hour to create and

five to ten minutes to upload. Two staff members who are proficient with PowerPoint work as designers for the screens. They include lots of graphics to enhance viewer appeal. The library's two cable channels continuously repeat a total of thirty screens. Approximately eight screens are added each month, and screens are updated or changed weekly.

Reference:	http://www.park-ridge.il.us
Project length:	Ongoing
Cost:	Library operating budget

Name:	**Portsmouth Computer Show**
Library:	Portsmouth Public Library
Contacts:	Susan Brough, children's librarian; Chris Fitt, program instructor
Address:	8 Islington St., Portsmouth, NH 03802
Phone:	(603) 427-1540
E-mail:	slbrough@lib.cityofportsmouth.com
Hardware:	5 computers, IBM compatible with Pentium and at least MMX capability; flatbed scanner; cameras (one per person)
Software:	MGI and Adobe Photo Deluxe
Description:	Library patrons ages 12 through adult were invited to create a computer slide show to celebrate the 375th birthday of their home city, Portsmouth, N.H., for library users to enjoy. Participants learned about photo and digital imaging, took photographs of the city, critiqued the images as a group, scanned the images, wrote text, and edited the results. The end product was a computer show of 21 images that can act as a screen saver. The images can be changed and updated as needed, and the entire show can be loaded into other computers using a Zip drive or CD. With 5 computers and 18 people, it was hard to give everyone enough time on the computer in a session. Three library staff members participated in the program.

Purchase of film and development of prints was paid for by the individual participants in this project. Depending on how many photos were processed per person, the cost could be approximately $20 or more each. Eighteen participants spent an estimated $400 total. The library paid $100 to the instructor, although he was willing to do the program for free. He devoted 12 hours of class time and perhaps another 6 at home planning and pulling things together, etc. The library owns the computers and scanner and purchased the software. Also, the instructor lent a couple of cameras to individuals who did not have them. |
| Project length: | July 1, 1998–August 1, 1998 |
| Cost: | $300–$500 including $100 for MGI and Adobe Photo Deluxe |

Reference

Reference projects cover the waterfront from wall charts to reference databases of local and community information. Some involve the Internet, but most are stand-alone projects within a single library. The Chesterfield County Public Library created a reader's advisory resources Web page that displays regularly updated library information such as book of the month, pathfinders, and recommended reading. The La Grange Park Public Library in cooperation with other agencies created a database with information on more than 270 community service and health care agencies. The Maywood Public Library used WordPerfect to create a simple database of 1,200 Dewey decimal numbers to produce a simple booklet and wall chart to assist patrons in locating information without librarian intervention. Other useful projects in this chapter include the Queens Borough Public Library's job information center, the Center of Business Information's virtual reference librarian, and the Center for Excellence in Disaster Management & Humanitarian Assistance's Nuclear, Biological, and Chemical Terrorist Event CD-ROM.

Name:	**Client Tracking Conversion**
Library:	Information Management Center, Baxter International
Contact:	Information Management Center
Address:	Rte. 120 & Wilson Rd., Round Lake, IL 60073
Phone:	(847) 270-5331; Fax: (847) 270-5381
Web site:	http://www.baxter.com
Hardware:	Network drive, staff PCs
Software:	Microsoft Access 97
Description:	Baxter International, Inc., is a global producer of biotechnology products such as those used in hospitals and other health care institutions. The library performs a host of services for company employees, including reference and database searching. Many different databases—some expensive—are available to employees

worldwide. The actual cost for online searches is charged back to the clients who request them. A way to track the information and the reference encounters has been in place for some time, but it has not worked efficiently. A new system was created with Microsoft Access 97, with customized forms for data entry and recall. Information about each search is recorded, including the department, amount of time online with the database, and date. The data is cumulated and reported to company accounting monthly.

The whole staff participated as test subjects and gave feedback. A major problem encountered was wanting to do more with the system than was technically known. This was solved with training and manuals.

Project length: Ongoing
Cost: None

Name: **Internet Web Site Index for Reference**
Library: Glenside Public Library District
Contact: Michael Moulds
Address: 25 E. Fullerton Ave., Glendale Heights, IL 60139
Phone: (630) 260-1550; Fax: (630) 260-1433
Hardware: Compaq USA PC
Software: Microsoft Word
Description: A much-used list of Web sites is maintained by the Glenside Public Library using Microsoft Word. The sites on the list are collected through recommendations from patrons and staff, newspaper and magazine articles, and from the librarians' online experience. It is maintained on disk and updated and printed out periodically. The current printed version is 40 pages. The list is simple in focus, including only the name of the Web site, subject, the date it was added to the list, and the Web address. No annotations are included. The library keeps one copy at the reference desk. Some of the types of information contained in the list include sites about telephone listings, African American history, employment, business, corporations, and many other hot topics.
Project length: July 1996–present
Cost: None

Name: **Job-Search Resources Booklets**
Library: Queens Borough Public Library Job Information Center
Contact: Robert Sage

Address:	89-11 Merrick Blvd., Jamaica, NY 11432
Phone:	(718) 846-0753
E-mail:	robertsag@queens.lib.ny.us
Hardware:	IBM PC, Hewlett Packard LaserJet 5P printer, Sharp photocopier
Software:	Microsoft Word
Description:	To cut down the search time required for answering the most frequently asked questions in the job information center (JIC), the JIC published a series of booklets entitled "Job Search Resources." These booklets are researched, edited, and formatted on a standard word processing program (Microsoft Word), then printed and distributed to the 62 branches of the Queens Library System entirely by the five staff members of the JIC. The format for all booklets is standardized, allowing a new update to be produced, printed, and distributed within a matter of days. This allows the timely nature of job search materials to be adjusted. The booklets have been very successful with the public. An interactive Web site featuring these booklets is now in development.
Reference:	ALA 1998 Poster Session, Washington, D.C.
Project length:	November 1997–present
Cost:	None

Name:	**The Nuclear, Biological, and Chemical Terrorist Events CD-ROM**
Organization:	Center of Excellence in Disaster Management & Humanitarian Assistance, Pacific Disaster Management Information Network (PDMIN) Information Resource Center
Contact:	Jan Zastrow, project manager
Address:	PDMIN, P.O. Box 235555, Honolulu, HI 96823-3509
Phone:	(808) 539-2545
E-mail:	zastrow@hawaii.edu
Hardware:	133 MHz IBM-compatible Pentium PC, several Apple Macintosh and Power Macintosh computers, QuickCAM and video cameras, recording decks, flatbed scanners, etc.
Software:	Microsoft Windows 95, Microsoft Office, Apple Media Tool, Apple QuickTime VR
Description:	The mission of the Center of Excellence in Disaster Management & Humanitarian Assistance is education, training, and research in operations other than war. The purpose of this project was to disseminate the information presented at a December 1996 center-hosted conference on medical consequence management of biological, chemical, radiation, and terrorist events to as wide an audience as possible by using interactive multimedia technology

as a distance learning medium. Conference lectures, tabletop exercises, and small-group sessions focused on crisis/consequence management and mitigation, giving many responsible for managing these events a first-ever opportunity to discuss the issues in detail.

The Nuclear, Biological, and Chemical Terrorist Events CD-ROM is the multimedia proceedings of that conference. It distills the content of the original program into an interactive learning opportunity, containing both the lectures and scenarios presented at the conference. Guided by an introductory navigational tutorial and context-sensitive help screens throughout, the student participates in the development of several scenarios by playing the role of a military agent, a civilian government responder, or a nongovernmental organization staffer, making choices and assessments based on the information provided. All 17 original conference lectures are presented in a condensed audio and text format, and topical webliographies—either for simultaneous, hyperlinked Internet access or to printout for later reference—are available as additional resources to enrich the learning experience. At any time during the "play," participants may test themselves to evaluate their understanding of the material and, when all 20 test questions are answered successfully, then print out a certificate of completion for continuing education credit.

An out-of-house vendor, Mind Expansion Technology (METECH), was hired to develop the graphics and 3D QuickTime components and to put all the pieces together. One of the toughest problems it encountered was developing on a Mac platform and then attempting to convert the product to full functionality for Windows-based PCs—unfortunate because the primary audience, the U.S. military, is virtually 100 percent PC. A hybrid product was actually needed—for both Macs and PCs—for this particular audience. Also, although all lectures and most components of the role-playing scenarios were developed in both audio and text formats (both readable and printable) for "audio-challenged" computers without speakers, the user still needed a sound card to run the CD. In hindsight, a nonaudio, text-only version for those without any audio capability should have been made.

The project manager's other activities took a back seat during the intensive three-month production period. The other three members of the staff were not directly affected until the week before the deadline, when all were drafted into full-time software testing. When the beta version was approved, any later changes had to be made as cost overruns. Unfortunately, the vendor was not able to solve printing and setup discrepancies in the PC version until long after the initial deadline. In hindsight, the product should have been developed in the same environment on which it will ultimately be used.

Despite frustration, setbacks, and moments of high anxiety, this interactive distance learning project was well worth undertaking. The CD-ROM has since become a highly acclaimed prototype in its field and has brought visibility and accolades to both the Pacific Disaster Management Information Network and the Center of Excellence.

References:	The Center of Excellence in Disaster Management & Humanitarian Assistance at http://coe.tamc.amedd.army.mil
	METECH—Mind Expansion Technology at http://www.metech.com
Project length:	Aug. 4, 1997–May 1998

Name:	**Public Inquiry Mail and Telephone Services Unit (PIMATS): Smithsonian Online**
Organization:	Smithsonian Institution
Contact:	Katherine Neill Ridgley, PIMATS manager
Address:	S1 Bldg., Rm. 153, Washington, DC 20560-0010
Phone:	(202) 357-2987; Fax: (202) 633-9353
E-mail:	info@info.si.edu
Hardware:	IBM PC compatible
Software:	Windows 95, WordPerfect, Microsoft Front Page
Description:	Established in the early 1970s, the Visitor Information and Associates' Reception Center (VIARC) seeks to broaden the public's knowledge, appreciation, and enjoyment of the Smithsonian and to facilitate and promote participation in its programs and activities. As a central support organization and the principal contact point for information about the Institution, which includes 16 museums, the National Zoo, and myriad research bureaus and offices, one of the ways in which VIARC's work is carried out is through the Public Inquiry Mail and Telephone Services Unit (PIMATS), which also performs outreach to the tourism industry.

The purpose of PIMATS is to handle inquiries from the public in an organized and cohesive manner and to promote the Smithsonian as a primary tourist destination in the nation's capital. With the assistance of volunteer information specialists, PIMATS today serves annually some 35,000 correspondents (postal and e-mail) and handles inquiries seven days a week from 350,000 telephone and TTY callers.

Staff from America Online (AOL) approached the Smithsonian in 1993, and a pilot group of four offices from around the Institution agreed to provide information to AOL members through Smithsonian Online. Thus, a new mechanism to achieve the Institution's mission to "increase and diffuse knowledge" was realized.

VIARC began by offering basic information on the scope and size of the Institution, planning a visit, volunteering, membership, and numerous Smithsonian-related topics ranging from identifying a Stradivarius violin to bibliographies on pandas and automobiles. An online inquiry service is also offered. VIARC now maintains Web sites with visitor planning, event, and exhibition information as well as an exciting site called Encyclopedia Smithsonian/FAQ. The site has received more than 550,000 hits and served more than 44,000 individual site visitors. The online inquiry assistance is still offered, and because of the more efficient manner in which inquiries are handled, less staff can process them more quickly. Information is also provided to two non-Smithsonian Web sites for the tour and travel industry: TravelFile, accessible to travel agents through their online airline reservations systems and to consumers via America Online and the Web, and NTA Online, available to members of the National Tour Association (group tour operators and those who supply them with services).

VIARC had a fiscal 1998 budget of $1,836,000, which included support for the Public Inquiry Mail and Telephone Information Services. There is a paid staff of 3 full-time and 1 part-time; volunteers (4 correspondence researchers, 1 indexer, 1 online material formatter/uploader, and 1 clerical). Telephone Information Service has a paid staff of 3 and 36 volunteers.

Reference:	http://www.si.edu.resource/faq/start.htm
Project length:	Online services mid-1993–present; May 1996–present
Cost:	Federal monies for computer equipment, software, and office supplies; staff salaries are covered by both federal and private funds

Name:	**Reader's Advisory Resources Web Page**
Library:	Chesterfield County Public Library
Contacts:	Neal Wyatt; Ginger Armstrong
Address:	P.O. Box 297, 9501 Lori Rd., Chesterfield, VA 23832
Phone:	(804) 768-7738 or (804) 768-7739
E-mail:	nyatt@vsla.edu
Hardware:	Dell Pentium desktop computer, Hewlett Packard LaserJet 4 Plus printer

Software:	HoTMetaL Pro 3
Description:	This project uses the World Wide Web to make library-related reader's advisory information available to people of all ages. The Web page is also used for staff development and for keeping current with trends in the literature. It consists of five interconnected Web pages: site of the month, book of the month, guide to the Web, pathfinders, and recommended reading. The core of the Web page is the site of the month, which combines Web sites with printed materials on a single topic. Complementing this is the book of the month page, an annotated page of books suggested for adults, children, and young adults covering fiction and nonfiction. Other sections guide users through the Web focusing on book-related sites and resources.

Collection Management highlights titles of note on the Web page for staff and patrons. The staff's reader's advisory newsletter, Ripples, and the collection management reader's advisory newsletter, Books & Bytes, are added to the page and allow library staff to promote titles on the Web.

It is suggested that anyone wishing to tackle a project like this should think about the relationships between the pages and create clear goals and descriptions for each Web section before beginning. The pages will be more cohesive, more creative, and better organized as a result. Updating on a monthly schedule can be time-consuming, so make sure the updating frequency chosen matches the actual amount of time that can be allotted to the project. The site takes two days each month to update.

If this project were started over, the guide would be limited to the Web section and would focus more on the reader's advisory portion of the page. It would also be mandated that all book lists that are included under pathfinders be annotated before they are loaded onto the page so that they will be of more benefit as a reader's advisory tool. |
| Project length: | January 1998–present |
| Cost: | None |

Name:	**Regional Libraries for Access to Community Services (ReLACS)**
Library:	La Grange Park Public Library in cooperation with the La Grange Public Library, Hodgkins Public Library, and West Suburban Chamber of Commerce
Contact:	Dixie Conkis

Address:	555 N. La Grange Rd., La Grange Park, IL 60526
Phone:	(708) 352-0100; Fax: (708) 352-1606
E-mail:	conkisd@sls.lib.il.us
Hardware:	Pentium 166 PC and multimedia computers
Software:	AskSam for Windows
Description:	The ReLACS database contains more than 270 community service and health care agencies that serve the residents and businesses of the La Grange Park, La Grange, Hodgkins, Countryside, Indian Head Park, and Willow Springs communities. It is also available on the Internet. The database was conceived in response to a health needs assessment study conducted by the Community Memorial Foundation that identified a need for the coordination of community services.

A consultant was hired to serve as project coordinator and to choose the software and set up the database structure. She then selected and contacted the organizations to be included. Once the information had been gathered, volunteers and staff at the La Grange Park Library entered the information into the database. This phase of the project had the greatest impact on the La Grange Park Library because many hours of work were required to complete this stage. Demonstrations of the database were then held, first for the staff of the other libraries and chamber of commerce, then for the organizations included.

A second consultant was hired to convert the database into HTML to make it available on the Internet. Because the software chosen did not have the capability automatically to convert to HTML, this became a long and complicated procedure.

The original plan had called for the information to be updated quarterly, but this entailed too much work because each organization had to be contacted. The organizations were split among the four agencies, and letters were sent out requesting updates. Those who did not respond were called. It was thereafter decided to update the database yearly. The ReLACS database has proved helpful to the community and has been used to answer questions at the reference desk.

References:	http://www.nsn.org/lpshome/relacs
	Suburban Library System Reference Newsletter, 15 Nov. 1997.
Project length:	October 1996–present
Cost:	$43,000, of which $20,000 came from a grant from the Illinois State Library using LSCA funding and $23,000 came from participating libraries and the West Suburban Chamber of Commerce

Name:	**Virtual Reference Librarian**
Library:	Woodruff Library Center for Business Information, Emory University Libraries
Contact:	Ruth A. Pagell
Address:	540 Ashbury Cir., Atlanta, GA 30322
Phone:	(404) 727-1112; Fax: (404) 727-1012
E-mail:	rpagell@emory.edu
Hardware:	IBM PC compatible 486 or higher, ISDN phone line, NT-1 device, telephone, AT&T Vistium Personal Video System
Software:	Applications sharing software, Windows 95; CD-ROM databases: F & SA Index Plus, Euromonitor International's marketing statistics, Dun's Million Dollar Disc
Description:	At the time of the project, the Goizueta Business Schools executive and evening MBA programs were located off campus, The business school itself is separate from the Center for Business Information. The goal of this project was to examine the applications of desktop video conferencing, using application shareware, in a reference library environment. The Center for Business Information, the Goizueta Business School at Emory University, and AT&T beta tested desktop video conferencing as a means to deliver distance reference service, including consultation, documentation, training, and sharing of CD-ROM databases.

The experiment used a two-monitor AT&T Vistium Personal Video System. One machine, with all of the software, resided in the library. The second machine first was placed in the lab of the Goizueta Business School building and then at an off-campus teaching location for executive and evening MBA students. Students stated their reference requests to the librarian. Each party saw an image of the other in a small area on the right side of the screen. In one scenario, after the desired information was identified through a traditional reference interview, the librarian could load the particular CD-ROM on which the requested information resided and turn control of the CD-ROM over to the student. In another situation, the librarian and the student together created a search strategy, writing it out on the white board.

The personal aspect of being able to visually and descriptively walk a student through a research session is a friendlier way than text-only online searching or a telephone research help desk. However, it was assumed that users would welcome the opportunity to see the staff; therefore, staff were surprised when some students actually covered the screen.

Challenges included coordinating the technology used among the library, the business school, and the university's telecommunications unit as well as with the vendor. The picture quality was grainy and was sensitive to the lighting of the area. It was important that only one person touched the mouse at one time, or the system tended to lock.

From a service perspective, use of the system had to be scheduled so that a librarian would be available.

Achievements included students' hands-on training on CD-ROMs rather than their coming into the library when staff would not be available. Also, the customized documentation created to assist students searching at remote locations was well worth the effort.

References: Diane Clark, "Reference Service Via Desktop Video Conferencing," 1997. Available at http://www.slis.ualberta.ca/598/dianec/videocon.htm

Ruth A. Pagell, "The Virtual Reference Librarian: Using Desktop Video Conferencing for Distance Reference," *Electronic Library* (Feb. 1996).

Russell Shaw, "AT&T & University Start Video Conferencing Test," *Newsbytes* (18 April 1995): 16.

Project length: February–May 1995

Cost: Hardware and software provided by what was then AT&T (now Lucent Technologies); cost of installing an ISDN line absorbed by the library and the business school

Name: **Wall Charts for Reference**
Library: Maywood Public Library District
Contact: Patrick Dewey, director
Address: 121 S. Fifth Ave., Maywood, IL 60153
Phone: (708) 343-1847; Fax: (708) 343-2115
E-mail: patrickdewey@hotmail.com
Hardware: IBM PC compatible
Software: WordPerfect 7
Description: A wall chart of Dewey decimal or LC numbers is an excellent way to assist many patrons searching for materials in the library. A surprisingly high percentage of questions from patrons can be answered in this manner. Producing a wall chart is a simple project, requiring a relatively small amount of time, material, and effort with almost any word processor.

The project began by collecting a list of subject headings and their corresponding Dewey numbers. Such information can be gathered in a variety of ways, including from a list of common questions or authoritative sources. It was decided, however, to take some of the information directly from the card catalog. (Since OPACs were installed, the card catalog, while still available, was no longer maintained or updated.) Librarians and clerks went through every drawer and listed the important subject headings with their Dewey numbers. Everyone used their professional judgment to determine useful subject headings; since the wall chart could contain only so many headings, it was necessary to select the most useful. The data was typed into a two-field document that was easy to sort. The document was then printed out and edited. The corrected disk was printed again and fastened to a hard posterboard surface for display at the ends of book shelves. The finished wall chart contains approximately 1,000 subject headings with their corresponding numbers.

Project length: January–April 1998
Cost: Minor printing costs and staff time

APPENDIX A

Computer Periodicals of Interest

Computer Life
Ziff-Davis Publishing Co.
135 Main St., 14th Fl.
San Francisco, CA 94105
(415) 357-5355
E-mail: ceditors@zd.com

Computer Shopper
Ziff-Davis Publishing Co.
One Park Ave., 11th Fl.
New York, NY 10016-3500
http://www.cshopper.com

Computer Weekly
Reed Business Publishing Group
Quadrant House
The Quadrant
Sutton SM2 3AS, Eng.
Fax: (0181) 652-8979
http://www.computerweekly.co.uk

Computers in Libraries
Information Today, Inc.
143 Old Marlton Pike
Medford, NJ 08055-6266
(609) 654-6266
Fax: (609) 654-4309

Home Office Computing
Scholastic, Inc.
411 Lafayette St., 4th Fl.
New York, NY 10003
(800) 866-5821
Fax: (212) 982-2886
E-mail: lettershoc@aol.com

InfoWorld
InfoWorld Publishing Co.
155 Bovet Rd., Ste. 800
San Mateo, CA 94402
(415) 572-7341
E-mail: letters@infoworld.com

Internet World
Meckler Corp.
20 Ketchum St.
Westport, CT 06880
(203) 226-6967
Fax: (203) 454-5840
E-mail: newbarth@iw.com

Library Software Review
Sage Publications, Inc.
2455 Teller Rd.
Thousand Oaks, CA 91320
(805) 499-9774
Fax: (805) 499-0871

Library Technology Reports
American Library Assn.
50 E. Huron St.
Chicago, IL 60611

MacUser
Ziff-Davis Publishing Co.
50 Tower Ln., 18th Fl.
Foster City, CA 94404
(415) 378-5600
E-mail: letters@macuser.com

NetGuide
CMPnet
P.O. Box 420355
Palm Coast, FL 32142-9371
(800) 829-0421 or (904) 445-4662
http://www.cmp.com

PC/Computing
Ziff-Davis Publishing Co.
50 Beale St., 13th Fl.
San Francisco, CA 94105
http://www.pccomputing.com

PC Magazine
Ziff-Davis Publishing Co.
One Park Ave.
New York, NY 10016-3500
E-mail: pcmaz@zd.com
http://www.pcmag.com

PC Week
Ziff-Davis Publishing Co.
20 Presidents Landing
Medford, MA 02155
(800) 451-1032 or (617) 393-3700
E-mail: PCW-L2ES@zd.com
http://www.pcweek.com

PC World
PC World Communications, Inc.
501 Second St., Ste. 600
San Francisco, CA 94107
(415) 243-0500
Fax: (415) 442-1891
E-mail: letters@pcworld.com
http://www.pcworld.com

San Jose Mercury News
Knight Ridder, Inc.
750 Ridder Park Dr.
San Jose, CA 95190
(408) 920-5000

Software and CD-ROM Reviews on File
Facts On File, Inc.
11 Penn Plaza, 15th Fl.
New York, NY 10001-2006
(212) 967-8800

Technology & Learning
Peter Li, Inc.
2451 E. River Rd.
Dayton, OH 45439
(513) 294-5785

Technology Connection
Linworth Publishing, Inc.
480 E. Wilson Bridge Rd., Ste. L
Worthington, OH 43085-2372
(614) 436-7107
Fax: (614) 436-9490
http://www.infomall.org/Showcase/Linworth

Windows Magazine
CMP Publications, Inc.
One Jericho Plaza
Jericho, NY 11753
(516) 562-5000
E-mail: winmag@cmp.com
http://www.winmag.com

APPENDIX B

Project Software

The descriptions in this appendix include the software librarians used in their projects. However, many other similar software packages could be substituted. Every effort has been made to include all of the programs from the text, but information on some could not be located. For more information about any software not listed in this appendix, contact the program's sponsoring library. In addition, the Internet provides access to many software evaluation sites.

Prices quoted are the most recent as of this writing. When no price is given, usually due to the variety of versions and configurations available, contact the vendor. Prices, software versions, and hardware requirements change frequently; therefore, it is important to contact the vendor directly for the latest prices and updates. Vendors' addresses are listed in appendix C.

A to Zap! (Ablac) is a children's educational program that teaches the alphabet to grades Pre-K through grade 1. It is available for Microsoft Windows 3.x. $59.99

Accent Professional for Windows (Accent) is a multilanguage word processing program for Windows that contains 170 fonts, 20 menu languages, and 50 virtual keyboards. It reproduces the accents and other marks for 30 languages.

Adobe PageMaker (Adobe Systems) is an advanced desktop publishing package. It includes page layouts for multipage documents of text and graphics. $895

Adobe PageMill (Adobe) is a complete design, build, post, and manage Web page software package available for Macintosh or Windows. $99

Adobe Photo Deluxe (Adobe) is a graphics package for digitizing and modifying a personal collection of photographs. Versions available for Macintosh or Windows. $39–$79

Adventure is the original computer text game. Players are introduced to a fascinating land where they move through an imaginary landscape, solve puzzles, and escape rat attacks. It is available on the Internet and in various bundles of computer games. Free

Alpha 4 (latest version is Alpha 5 for Windows by Alpha Software) is a work group and desktop database that can handle field and index names up to 32 characters in length. $99

Apache (Apache Software Foundation) consists of a variety of JAVA-related tools and JAVA-enhancement software.

Apple Media Tool (Apple Computer), available for Apple Macintosh and Power Mac/System 7.1, is a multimedia authoring package that does not require scripting to use specialized fonts, graphics, and sound files. $495

Apple QuickTime VR Authoring Studio (Apple Computer) is a multimedia tool for Web and other design work. It creates panoramas and objects. Program components include Panorama Stitcher, Panorama Maker, Object Maker, Scene Maker, and Project Maker. It is available for Apple Macintosh and Power Mac. $395

AppleShare (Claris) is a file- and print-sharing program available for Macintosh or Windows.

AskSam for Windows (askSam Systems) is a database system that contains word-processing, text-retrieval, and database components. Information may be entered and used as structured data or unstructured data. Typical uses include bibliographies, name and address files, HTML documents, etc. It is available for Windows 95, Windows 3.x, Windows NT, Windows for Workgroups, Novell NetWare. $150 for version 3.0; $1,495–$15,000 for network version

Authorware (Prentice-Hall New Media) is a presentation authoring system for stand-alone multimedia training programs for the Macintosh computer and Windows PCs. It comes with three projects, a test generator, and online documentation. $149.95

B&T Link (Baker and Taylor) is a software package that let users order materials directly online from Baker and Taylor, a library materials jobber.

CALI (Computer-Assisted Legal Instruction) CD-ROM (The Center for Computer-Assisted Legal Instruction) contains exercises in 26 areas of the law. It is written by law professors. $39.95

Career English (Tutorsystems) is available as part of a kit that also contains The American Heritage Talking Dictionary, Basic Skills Series, and the Career English Series for $495. Site license alone, $3,750

Chicago Tribune (Newsbank) is a full-text (no images) CD-ROM database. Each CD-ROM contains one full year of newspaper text. $798 national; $348 regional

Cinahl (Cinahl Information Systems) is a database that covers nursing and allied health literature and information from 1982 to the present.

Appendix B **123**

ClarisWorks (Claris) is a program that encompasses most office requirements including spreadsheet, word processing, database management, drawing, and communications. It can be used to prepare and print reports, including visual multimedia presentations and slide shows.

CollegeSource (Career Guidance Foundation) is a CD-ROM and online product that contains the full information from more than 10,000 college catalogs. $798

Columbia Library System (Columbia Computing Services) is an integrated library circulation system. Main module, $1,095

Congressional Masterfile (Congressional Information Service) consists of two retrospective congressional indexes: 1789–1969 and 1970–present.

Contemporary Authors (SilverPlatter) is a Gale Research CD-ROM database that contains biographical information on more than 100,000 modern novelists, playwrights, nonfiction writers, journalists, and scriptwriters. The information is from the more than 100 print volumes of *Contemporary Authors*. $3,650

Core Biomedical Collection (Ovid) includes the full text of 15 major medical journals including the *American Journal of Medicine, New England Journal of Medicine*, and *JAMA: The Journal of the American Medical Association*. It is available in several formats, including CD-ROM and online.

Corel Classic Literature (Corel) is a multimedia CD-ROM that contains more than 3,000 historical and public domain documents. It is excellent as a general basic library. $2,495

Corel Draw (Corel) is a graphics-production package that includes page layout and design available in different Windows and Macintosh versions. $100–$500

Curious George (Houghton Mifflin Interactive), based on the books by the same name, is an entertaining and educational program for ages 3–6. $35

Current Biography (H. W. Wilson) is a CD-ROM product that contains more than 14,000 biographies and 8,500 obituaries (1940 to present). It is available in DOS, Macintosh, and Windows formats or online through the Internet.

Cyber Patrol (The Learning Company) is an Internet filtering system for use with Windows 3.x, Windows 95, or Apple Macintosh. Web areas are blocked by site. Access to the Internet may be restricted by time of day, total time spent on line per day or week, etc. $29.95

Dangerous Animals (Microsoft) is a Windows screen saver.

dBase for DOS (Borland International) is a popular database management system compatible with DOS-based PCs.

Dr. Seuss's ABCs (TLC Superstore) is based on Dr. Seuss's books, involving rhyme and character interaction. It is for grades two through five. It is compatible with Macintosh and Windows PCs. $14.95

Dun's Million Dollar Disc (Dun's Marketing Service) is a database of company corporate names and trade names, private or public status, trading exchange for public companies, SIC codes, import and export status, annual sales and employee counts, and key banking and accounting relationships. It is compatible with MS-DOS. $4,995

Electric Library (Infonautics) is a popular Internet database of millions of full-text articles, images, and speeches. It is useful for student research and general exploration.

Ellis Intro (The Center for Computer-Assisted Legal Instruction) is an English-language tutorial that includes grammar, vocabulary and cultural tutorials, listening and pronunciation tools, role-playing scenarios, context-sensitive translation, mastery tests, and skills tracking. There are more than 300 hours of instruction. Three separate series (Senior, Middle, and Intro) are priced differently. $39.95

Encyclopedia Americana on CD-ROM (Grolier Electronic Publishing) is the electronic version of the print encyclopedia available for PC or Macintosh. $179

English Vocabulary (Delta-Systems) is an English as a second language study package.

EOS International GLAS Series (Electronic Online Systems International) (Graphical Library Automation System) is a Windows-based library automation system. Main unit, $2,950

EOS International Managers Series 7.1 (Electronic Online Systems, International) is a library automation package.

Eudora Pro E-mail for Windows, Eudora Pro E-mail for Macintosh, and **Eudora Pro E-mail for Windows 95** and **Windows NT** (Qualcomm) are sophisticated e-mail packages with message filtering, attachments, and Internet connections between Macs and PCs. $29.95 and up

Excite (Excite, Inc.) is an Internet search engine available through any Internet browser.

F & SA Index Plus (InfoTrac) is a database that provides in-depth information on companies, industries, markets, and products worldwide.

FileMaker Pro (FileMaker) is a multiuser database management system. It can be used for many common functions, including the creation of reports, forms, mailing labels, graphics, etc. Both packages contain 40 ready-made project templates. $199

Appendix B

FirstSearch Core and Specialized Databases (OCLC) is an online subscription search service that contains up to 70 different databases.

Focus on Grammar—ESL (Exceller Software Corp.) is a Windows 3.x and Apple Macintosh tutorial program for English as a second language (ESL) students. It contains listening, reading, and writing exercises in four modules: basic, intermediate, high intermediate, and advanced. $99, each module

FoolProof Desktop Security (SmartStuff Software) is a Macintosh computer security program. It will direct file saving and lock control panels. It also protects the hard drive while allowing access to finder, CD-ROMs, and a network. $39–$589

Fortres 101 (Fortres Grand) is a computer security program for computers being used by more than one person or by students or the general public. It provides protection against users making unwanted changes to the operating system, Windows options, and many other parameters. Price varies according to site license.

FoxPro (now Visual FoxPro, by Microsoft) is an advanced sophisticated database management system compatible with Apple Macintosh and Windows-based PCs. $499; $199 for standard edition

Fun with a Purpose (Creative Multimedia) is an educational package for Windows or Macintosh that features puzzles, characters, and other activities from *Highlights* magazine. $29.95

Googol Math Games (Paul T. Dawson) is a set of six math games for young people available as shareware over the Internet. $10 registration fee

Grolier Multimedia Encyclopedia (Grolier Electronic Publishing) is a true multimedia product for Windows or Macintosh with videos, audio, photos, and thousands of articles. $395

Harvest (developed by the Internet Research Task Force Research Group on Resource Discovery [IRTF-RD]) is a set of utilities that gather, extract, organize, search, cache, and replicate relevant information across the Internet. Further information is available at http://www.tardis.ed.ac.uk/harvest

Health Reference Center (Information Access) is a general database of 300 journals (150 full text) intended for use with the general public. $2,500

HealthStar (National Library of Medicine) provides bibliographic citations to the published literature covering health care delivery and administration as well as technology and research.

Hijack Pro 2.0 (International Microcomputer Software) is a Windows 95 and Windows NT file management system for graphics files. It can be used to manipulate graphics in a variety of ways, including converting, rendering, searching, thumb nailing, cataloging, scanning, importing and exporting, etc. More than 85 file formats are supported. $169

HoTMetaL and HoTMetaL Pro (SoftQuad) are hypertext, multimedia Web authoring systems. They work with Microsoft Internet Explorer, Netscape, Mosaic, etc., and are compatible with Windows 95 and Windows NT. $159

HTML Assistant Pro (Brooklyn North Software Works) is an HTML editor that contains a collection of assistance programs. These contain spell check, auto replace, and dialog boxes for placement of HTML tags. $99.95

IMAP (Internet Message Access Protocol) Mail Client (URLi) is an Internet e-mail program that provides enhancements over traditional Internet e-mail such as POP (Post Office Protocol). Free online

InfoTrac Databases (Information Access) is a series of CD-ROM databases.

InfoTrac Search Bank (Information Access) is an online product of Internet databases.

Just Grandma and Me (Broderbund) is an excellent program for children in kindergarten through third grade. Based on the book by Mercer Mayer, this program consists of several screens that are identical to those in the book. These may be explored by children for hot spots containing fun activities. The book comes to life with animation and sounds. The school edition contains 15 lesson plans for language arts, reading, writing, math, and science. $49.95 school edition; $99 lab pack

LegalTrac (Information Access) is an index for legal information of more than 800 publications. $3,500

LEXIS-NEXIS Databases (LEXIS-NEXIS) include a variety of legal service information. Some of the highlights include the full text of reported cases from the last 50 years; the full text of federal and state statutes; some federal and state administrative and regulatory materials; and a collection of secondary legal authorities such as encyclopedias, restatements, and law reviews.

Library Automation System (Data Research Associates) is an automated library system.

Lifetime Library (Learning 2000) is a massive instructional set of multiple CDs that cover reading, writing, and math. It can be used for GED or general educational needs for many age groups. It includes 11,000 question screens, 22,200 full-motion videos, 3,000 minutes of narrative text, thousands of photographs, 7,000 instructional screens, and 23 gigabytes of information. $599.99; individual units (Math, Algebra, and Reading & Writing) $249.99 each

Linux (Red Hat Software) is an operating system. Web: http://www.redhat.com/redhat/linuxinfo.html

Living Books (The Learning Company) contains titles that were all developed for the younger grades. Some of the best known titles are *Just Grandma and Me* and several based on Dr. Seuss stories. They are the ultimate in children's computerized pop-up interactive fiction and are also fun for adults. Prices vary per individual title; set of two titles, $179.95; complete collection, $375

Lotus 1-2-3 *See* Lotus SmartSuite

Lotus SmartSuite (Lotus Development) contains five major applications: Ami Pro 3.1, 1-2-3 Release 5, spreadsheet, Approach 3.0 database, Freelance Graphics presentation package, and the Organizer personal information manager. It is available for Windows 3.x. $540

McAfee VirusScan (McAfee Associates) is an antivirus program. $65 for Windows 95 and Windows NT; $29.95 for Apple Macintosh

MacGraphics Interface (MGX MacGraphics) is a graphics creation package for making sophisticated brochures, Web site development, logos, etc.

Magic School Bus (Microsoft) is a series of software products that include educational imaginary trips to visit dinosaurs, the solar system, the human body (a drive through), a rainforest, the ocean, and other places. $24.95 per unit

Massachusetts Administrative Law Library (Paul T. Dawson) is a collection of agency decisions for Windows or Macintosh computers. $100/year

Master Pronunciation (Outbound Train) is an English-language instruction system in 28 languages. It contains animated graphics for placement of the tongue, teeth, and lips for proper pronunciation. $695

Masterplots (EBSCO Publishing) is a CD-ROM that contains the information from the print version of the title. $1,295

Mavis Beacon Teaches Typing (Mindscape) is a typing tutorial compatible with Windows 95 and Windows 3.x. $39.95

Mavis Beacon Typing Tutor (Mindscape) is a typing tutorial for Macs.

MEDLINE (National Library of Medicine) is the online version of the database MEDlars (MEDlars onLINE). It covers the fields of veterinary medicine, the health care system, and the preclinical sciences and contains bibliographic citations and author abstracts, with 9 million records dating back to 1966. Each month 33,000 new citations are added.

Menu Builder (Carl) is a program that allows libraries to convert all of their software to a single graphical interface. Patrons can browse protected data. It includes password protection, third-party icons, data logging, and a revised menuing screen. It can be used for browser applications, online public access catalogs, and CD-ROM products. The program requires a 486dx or Pentium processor with Windows 3.1, 95, or NT 4.0, 16 MB RAM. $49.95 each for up to 25 workstations; $44.95 each for 26–50 workstations; $39.95 each for 51–75 workstations; $34.95 each for 76–100 workstations; $29.95 each for 101–150 workstations; $24.95 each for 151–200 workstations; cost for more than 200 workstations is available upon request

Microsoft Access 97 (Microsoft) is an Internet-ready database management system. It imports directly to external HTML tables and retrieves tables that use HTTP or FTP files. $339

Microsoft Encarta (Microsoft) is an excellent multimedia encyclopedia on CD-ROM. It consists of more than 30,000 articles and 300,000 links to Web information. $39.95

Microsoft Excel (Microsoft) is an advanced spreadsheet program, currently the most popular in the marketplace. $339

Microsoft FrontPage 98 (Microsoft) is a Web site construction tool. It includes an HTML editor and is compatible with Windows 3.x, Windows 95, and Windows NT. $500–$800

Microsoft Index Server 2.0 (Microsoft) works with Microsoft Information Server to index Internet and Intranet sites. A search may be made for Word text documents, Excel spreadsheet statistics, or HTML information.

Microsoft Internet Explorer 4.0 (Microsoft) is an Internet browser package that comes preinstalled on many computers. The system is compatible with Windows PCs and Apple Macintosh.

Microsoft Office (Microsoft) combines word processing, text editing, spreadsheet, and presentation graphics all in one package. $899 for Windows; $499 for Macintosh; $599 for gold edition

Microsoft Outlook (Microsoft) is a desktop information manager that assists with desktop information organization, Microsoft Office applications, and communications. It is compatible with Windows 95 and Windows NT. $81

Microsoft PowerPoint 4.0 (Microsoft) is a Windows 95/NT and Macintosh computer presentation package that works with overhead transparencies, flip charts, handouts, and 35mm slide layouts. It includes a clip art library of 1,000 images. $395 for Macintosh; $339 for Windows

Microsoft Publisher 98 and **Microsoft Publisher CD Deluxe** (Microsoft) is an advanced desktop publishing package used to produce online or hard copy products of text and graphics. Users can create newsletters, fliers, labels, signs, brochures, banners, stationary, etc. $79.95

Microsoft Windows 3.1, Windows 95, Windows 98, and **Windows NT** (Microsoft) are all versions of the same operating system. NT is an advanced system for local area network control.

Microsoft Windows for Workgroups 3.11 (Microsoft) is a network operating system that includes resource sharing, scheduling, and e-mail for Windows PCs. $440

Microsoft Windows NT Server 4.0 (Microsoft) is a network software package that has Windows 95 as the user interface. It is the basis for many business applications. It supports Novell Netware, AppleTalk, LAN Manager, NFS, TCP/IP, X.25, Windows for Workgroups. $809 for 5 users; $1,129 for 10 users

Microsoft Word (Microsoft) is an advanced word processing system available for Windows, Macintosh, and DOS computers. $339

Microsoft WordPad (Microsoft) is a low-end text editor that is built into the Windows operating system.

Microsoft Works (Microsoft) is an advanced work package that incorporates a spreadsheet, database system, and word processing program into one integrated desktop. It is compatible with the Apple Macintosh and Windows-based computers. $39

Middle Mastery (Outbound Train) is an English language and instruction system. $500 for the management system; $895 for a station license

Millie's Math House (Edmark), available in English and Spanish, is a math tutorial for ages 2–6. The game-like program has six main activities: Little, Middle & Big; Mouse House; Bing & Boing; Build-a-Bug; Number Machine; and Cookie Factory. Versions are available for Windows and Mac computers. $19.95, home version; $59.95, school version

My First Amazing World Explorer (Microsoft) is an educational program that contains five separate games. Children explore the world using a map and other tools. $35

Netscape Communicator (Netscape Communications) is an Internet Web browser with e-mail, conferencing, and Web publishing components. Free

Netscape Navigator 4.0 (Netscape Communications) is an Internet browser package that is compatible with Windows PCs and Apple Macintosh. It comes preinstalled on many computers and can also be downloaded through the Internet. Free

Newsbank Databases (Newsbank) is a collection of databases that include major city newspapers such as the *Chicago Tribune* on a CD-ROM. $1,000 and up/year

Norton Utilities (Symantec) is a disk drive utility that performs file optimization such as defragmentation, backup, data recovery, file protection, diagnostics, and repair. It works on drives up to two gigabytes and repairs corrupted files for WordPerfect, dBase, Excel, and Quattro Pro. $79.95; $99 for Macintosh version 3.5; $79 for Windows 95; $99 for Windows NT

Nursing Collection (Ovid) contains the full text of 15 leading journals in general and specialized nursing fields. Hypertext links to MEDLINE bibliographic database and the CORE Biomedical Collection are also included.

OmniPage Pro (Caere) is optical character recognition software used to scan and process documents for word processing. Windows and Macintosh versions are available. $499

Paintshop Pro (Jasc Software) is a graphics system that supplies photo retouching, painting, screen capture, and image format conversion for Windows PCs. The system supports more than 30 file formats. $99

Appendix B

PC-File (Outlook Software) is a database management system with dBase index compatibility and many high-level features. It allows up to 250 fields. Files may be imported and exported with WordPerfect, Microsoft Word, DIF, SDF, Excel, Lotus, and user-defined formats. $130 for single user; $399.95 for multiuser

Perl is a high-level programming language originally written by Larry Wall. It is free and supported only by its users. Further information may be obtained at http://www.perl.com.

Peter Rabbit (Mindscape) is an educational program for young children. $14.95

PI Kiosk Electronic Branch Library (Public Information Kiosk) is a turnkey computer system that provides library-chosen Web-based information at individual locations, similar to a cash station.

Pine E-mail is a UNIX-based e-mail package.

PolyView and **PolyView Screensaver** (PolyBites). Web: http://www.kagi.com/authors/polybytes/default.html $25

Print Shop (Broderbund), available for Macintosh and Windows computers, is a very popular outstanding graphics program for creating fliers, posters, invitations, greeting cards, calendars, banners, etc. It comes with a variety of fonts, templates, clip art, and boilerplates for projects. $79.95

ProCite for Windows (Research Information Systems) is a tool for managing and using bibliographies and reference databases. Bibliographies may be created in various styles. The system is compatible with Microsoft Word or WordPerfect. It is available for Windows 95 and Windows NT. $395

Quarterdeck Web Server 1 (Quarterdeck) is a multitasking software package that receives, manages, and searches for Web documents for Windows-based computers. It will process up to 25,000 requests per hour. $173

Quattro Pro (Corel) is a spreadsheet included as part of WordPerfect.

QUEST (Centura Software) is a data access tool for simple query language databases. $595

QuickBooks (Intuit) is a basic accounting package with invoicing, accounts receivable and aging, accounts payable, cash flow forecasts, profit and loss, balance sheet, custom reports, multiple time periods, contact management, to-do list, mail merge, and other features. $119 for QuickBooks version 5.0, Windows 3.x; $159.95 for QuickBooks for DOS 2.1; $129 for Windows CD-ROM Deluxe; $189 for QuickBooks Pro version 5.0 for Apple Macintosh/System 7 and Windows 3.x

Quicken (Intuit) is an easy-to-use financial planner for home or small business use. It is compatible with Apple Macintosh and Windows 3.x, Windows 95, and Windows NT. $59.95

Appendix B **131**

Reader's Guide (H. W. Wilson) is a monthly CD-ROM subscription that contains indexing to more than 240 general interest periodicals. $1,095

Ready, Set, Go (Abbott Systems) is a desktop publishing system for Apple Macintosh or Power Mac for the small home or small business office. It is used to create fliers, brochures, newsletters, letterheads, labels, invoices, etc. It includes spell check, search and replace text, and other features. $159

Safe-Pay Connection (Advantage Payroll Services) is a package for transmitting payroll information over a modem.

Sammy's Science House (Edmark) is an early-learning package (grades PreK–2) that is used to teach elementary science concepts. $59.95

School Mom (Motes Educational Software) is an educational program for ages 6–14. It includes teaching elements for math, the alphabet, spelling, English, and time. It is compatible with Windows 95 and Windows 98.

SilverPlatter's F & S Index Plus (SilverPlatter) provides detailed business and industry data such as sales, trend analysis, new product information, demographics, market strategies, etc. $2,500

SIRS Government Reporter CD-ROM (SIRS) is a database that includes information about domestic and international affairs, members of the U.S. Congress, historical documents, and much more in six separate databases. $800 for annual license

SIRS (Social Issues Resources Series) Researcher (SIRS) is a database of thousands of well-organized and easily searchable full-text articles from more than 1,200 journals from 1988 to the present geared to students doing research and term papers. $1,450

Synchronize (Qdea) is a utility for people who use more than one Macintosh computer at a time. Files are "synchronized" by automatically being copied from one Macintosh computer folder to another Macintosh or to a disk or server. This program copies the newest versions of files for an update. $29.95

Synchronize! Pro (Qdea) is a file transfer utility that performs mirroring activities for AppleShare file servers. $99.95

The Tortoise and the Hare (The Learning Company) is part of the Living Book series designed for younger grades. Children can interact with this lively computer program as they follow the traditional story. It is available for Macintosh or Windows. $19.95

Typing Made Easy (QED Information Sciences) is a typing tutorial program. $49.95

United Nations Treaty Index (William S. Hein) is a database of treaties and international agreements registered with the Secretariat of the United Nations. $495 for a two-release subscription

Uview (CineGraphics) is a universal viewer for specialized documents, especially 3-D graphics.

ViaGrafix Training Videos (ViaGrafix) is a series of videotapes that provides instruction in many areas of computer education, including most major Microsoft applications (Outlook, Word, Project, Office, Excel, PowerPoint, Windows, etc.), WordPerfect, Adobe PageMaker, and many others. About $50 per video

VirusScan (McAfee) is an antivirus program that detects and eliminates viruses from Windows 95-based PCs and Apple Macintosh computers. $65 for Windows 95 version; $29.95 for Macintosh version

WebSTAR 2.1 (StarNine Technologies) is a Web server package. It is used to capture relevant customer marketing information, distribute catalogs and price lists, and provide security. $399; $499 WebSTAR for the Macintosh

WESTLAW (WESTLAW) is a variety of databases for the legal world. There are more than 4,200 products under this name.

Winnie the Pooh and the Honey Tree (Edutainment Catalog) is a program for children ages 3–8 that is modeled after the famous storybook character. It is compatible with Windows and Macintosh computers. $30

WinSelect (HyperTechnologies) is a computer security program that gives the user great control over which files and programs may be accessed. It is an excellent tool for public access computer areas. $40–$5,000, depending upon the number of CPUs in the license

WinSelect Ikiosk (Carl) is a Windows 95 compatible program that allows users complete control over their Internet browser. Its features include import, export, autoload configurations, and authorized and unauthorized URL location box entries. It is also available for Windows 3.1 as Ikiosk. Price based on site license

WinU (Bardon Data Systems) is a computer security system that provides an access control menu. Time limits may be set for the use of any program or desktop component. The user is given warning and a grace period prior to program shutdown. It is compatible with Windows 95. $49.95

WordPerfect 6.0, 6.1, 7.0, 8.0, and **9.0** (Corel) is an outstanding, full-featured word processing system with a multitude of included features such as Quattro Pro, a spreadsheet, an easy-to-use database sort function, address book, Grammatik, and spell check. The more recent the version, the more powerful and easier it is to use. DOS and Windows versions are available. Prices vary; consult with the company or a local vendor

WS_FTP (Ipswitch) is a file transfer program for sending files to and from an Internet server directory when updating or creating Web pages. $100

APPENDIX C

Computer Software Companies

Abbott Systems, Inc.
62 Mountain Rd.
Pleasantville, NY 10570
(800) 552-9157 or (914) 747-4171
Fax: (914) 747-9115

Ablac Learning Works, Ltd.
South Devon House
Newton Abbott Devon UK
 TQ12 2BP
(01626) 332233
Fax: (01626) 331464
E-mail: educ@ablac.co.uk
http://www.ablac.co.uk/a

Accent Software International, Ltd.
2864 S. Circle Dr., Ste. 340
Colorado Springs, CO 80906
(719) 576-2604
Fax: (719) 576-2604

Adobe Systems, Inc.
345 Park Ave.
San Jose, CA 95110-2704
(800) 833-6687 or (408) 536-6000
Fax: (408) 537-6000

Advantage Payroll Services
P.O. Box 1966
Auburn, ME 04211-1966
(630) 628-1966
http://www.advantagepayroll.com

Alpha Software Corp.
168 Middlesex Tpk.
Burlington, MA 01803
(800) 945-8565
Fax: (617) 272-4876
http://www.alphasoftware.com

Apache Software Foundation
c/o Covalent Technologies, Inc.
1200 N St., Ste. 112
Lincoln, NE 68508
http://www.apache.org

Apple Computer Inc.
1 Infinite Loop
Cupertino, CA 95014
(800) 776-2333 or (408) 996-1010
http://www.apple.com

askSam Systems
P. O. Box 1428
Perry, FL 32347
(800) 327-5726
http://www.asksam.com

Baker & Taylor
2709 Water Ridge Pkwy.
Charlotte, NC 28217
(800) 775-1800
Fax: (908) 429-4037
http://www.baker-taylor.com

Bardon Data Systems
1164 Solano Ave., Ste. 415
Albany, CA 94706-1639
(510) 526-8470
Fax: (510) 526-1271

Borland International, Inc.
100 Borland Way
Scotts Valley, CA 95066-3249
(800) 233-2444 or (408) 431-1000
Fax: (408) 431-4122
http://www.borland.com

Broderbund
500 Redwood Blvd.
Novato, CA 94948
(800) 521-6263 or (415) 382-4400
Fax: (415) 382-4419
http://www.broderbund.com/

Brooklyn North Software Works, Inc.
One Tech Dr.
Andover, MA 01810
(800) 349-1422 or (619) 560-8051
Fax: (978) 557-0007
http://www.brooknorth.com

1969 Upper Water St., Ste. 1703
Halifax, NS B3J 3R7 Canada
(800) 349-1422 or (902) 425-0900
Fax: (902) 425-0731

Caere Corp.
100 Cooper Court
Los Gatos, CA 95030
(800) 535-7226 or (408) 395-7000
Fax: (408) 354-2743

Career Guidance Foundation
8090 Engineer Rd.
San Diego, CA 92111
(800) 854-2670

Carl Corp.
3801 E. Florida, Ste. 300
Denver, CO 80210
(303) 758-3030
Fax: (303) 758-0606
http://www.carl.org

Center for Computer-Assisted Legal Instruction
565 W. Adams St.
Chicago, IL 60661
(312) 906-5348
http://www.cali.org

Centura Software Corp.
1060 Marsh Rd.
Menlo Park, CA 94025
(800) 876-3267 or (650) 321-9500
Fax: (650) 321-5471

Cinahl Information Systems
1509 Wilson Terr.
Glendale, CA 91206
(800) 959-7167
E-mail: cinahl@cinahl.com
http://www.cinahl.com

CineGraphics
2317 Falkirk Row
La Jolla, CA 92037
(858) 513-1440
Fax: (858) 513-1444
E-mail: info@cinegraphics.net
http://www.cinegraphics.net

Claris Corp.
5201 Patrick Henry Dr.
P. O. Box 58168
Santa Clara, CA 95052-8168
(800) 544-8554
Fax: (408) 987-7460
http://www.grolier.com

CMP Media, Inc.
225 N. Michigan Ave., Ste. 2516
Chicago, IL 60601
(312) 946-6600
http://www.cmp.com

Columbia Computing Services
8101 E. Prentice Ave., Ste. 700
Englewood, CO 80111
(800) 663-0544

Congressional Information Service, Inc.
4520 East-West Highway
Bethesda, MD 20814-3389
(800) 638-8380 or (301) 654-1550
Fax: (301) 654-4033
E-mail: cisinfo@lexis-nexis.com
http://www.cispubs.com

Corel Corp.
1600 Carling Ave.
The Corel Bldg.
Ottawa, ON K1Z 8R7 Canada
(800) 772-6735 or (613) 728-8200
Fax: (613) 728-9790
http://www.corel.com

Creative Multimedia Corp.
225 Broadway SW, Ste. 600
Portland, OR 97205
(503) 241-4351
Fax: (503) 241-4370

Data Research Associates, Inc.
1276 N. Warson Rd.
St. Louis, MO 63132-1806
(800) 325-0888 or (314) 432-1100
Fax: (314) 993-8927
E-mail: Sales@DRA.COM
http://www.dra.com

Delta Systems Co., Inc.
1400 Miller Pkwy.
McHenry, IL 60050-7030
(800) 323-8270 or (815) 363-3582
Fax: (800) 909-9901 or
   (815) 363-2948
http://www.delta-systems.com

DK Multimedia Inc.
95 Madison Ave.
New York, NY 10016
(212) 213-4800
Fax: (212) 213-5240
http://www.dkmultimedia.com

Dun's Marketing Service
Three Sylvan Way
Parsippany, NJ 07054-3896
(201) 605-6000
Fax: (201) 605-6911
http://cd-rom-guide.com/cdprod1/
   cdhrec/002/302.shtml

EBSCO Publishing
P.O. Box 2250
Peabody, MA 01960
(508) 535-8500
Fax: (508) 535-8545

Edmark Corp.
P. O. Box 97021
Redmond, WA 98073-9721
(800) 691-2986 or (425) 556-8400
E-mail: edmarkteam@
 edmark.com
http://edmark.com

Edutainment Catalog
1700 Progress Dr.
Hiawatha, IA 52233
(800) 338-3844
Fax: (800) 226-1942
E-mail: edutainco@
 tecdirectinc.com
http://www.edutainco.com

Electronic Online Systems International
5838 Edison Pl.
Barnesville, MN 56514-0100
(800) 752-4243, (800) 876-5484,
 or (619) 431-8400
Fax: (619) 431-8448

Euromonitor International, Ltd.
122 S. Michigan Ave., Ste. 1200
Chicago, IL 60603
(312) 922-1157
Fax: (312) 922-1157
http://www.euromonitor.com

Exceller Software Corp.
2 Graham Rd. W
Ithaca, NY 14850
(607) 257-5634
Fax: (607) 257-1665

FileMaker, Inc.
5301 Patrick Henry Dr.
P.O. Box 58168
Santa Clara, CA 95052-8168
(800) 325-2747
Fax: (408) 987-3932
http://www.claris.com

Fortres Grand Corp.
P.O. Box 888
Plymouth, IN 46563
(800) 331-0372 or (219) 935-3891
Fax: (800) 882-4381
http://www.fortres.com

Gale Research
27500 Drake Rd.
Farmington Hills, MI 48331-3535
(800) 877-4253
Fax: (800) 414-5043
http://www.gale.com

GenText, Inc.
9400 N. Central Expressway,
 Ste. 1640
Dallas, TX 75231-5045
(214) 365-0421
Fax: (214) 365-0591

Grolier Electronic Publishing
90 Sherman Tpk.
Danbury, CT 06816
(800) 6121-1115 or (203) 797-3500
Fax: (203) 797-3197
http://www.grolier.com

H. W. Wilson
950 University Ave.
Bronx, NY 10452-4224
(800) 367-6770 or (212) 588-8400
http://www.hwwilson.com

Harvest Team
http://www.ccu.edu.tw/doc/
 harvest/teamcontact.html

Houghton Mifflin Interactive
120 Beacon St.
Somerville, MA 02143
(617) 503-4800
Fax: (617) 503-4900
http://www.hminet.com

Hyper Technologies, Inc.
1125 Fir Ave.
Blaine, WA 98230
(800) 663-8381
Fax: (604) 464-8680
Email: dkirk@hypertec.com
http://www.hypertec.com

Infonautics Corp.
900 W. Valley Rd., Ste. 1000
Waynem, PA 19087-1830
(610) 971-8840

Information Access Co.
362 Lakeside Dr.
Foster City, CA 94404
(800) 227-8431 or (415) 378-5200
http://library.iacnet.com

InfoTrac
see Information Access Co.

InterBase Software Corp.
100 Enterprise Way
Scotts Valley, CA 95066-3249
(800) 632-2864
Fax: (831) 431-4142
http://www.interbase.com

International Microcomputer Software, Inc.
1895 Francisco Blvd. E
San Rafael, CA 94901-5506
(800) 833-4674 or (415) 257-3000
Fax: (415) 257-3565
http://www.imsisoft.com

Intuit, Inc.
P.O. Box 7850
Mountain View, CA 94039-7850
(800) 446-8848 or (650) 944-6000
Fax: (650) 322-1597
http://www.intuit.com

Ipswitch, Inc.
81 Hartwell Ave.
Lexington, MA 01273
(617) 676-5700
Fax: (617) 676-5710
E-mail: info@ipswitch.com
http://www.ipswitch.com

Jasc Software, Inc.
P.O. Box 44997
Eden Prairie, MN 55344
(800) 622-2793 or (612) 930-9800
Fax: (612) 930-9172
http://www.jasc.com

Jostens Learning Corp.
9920 Pacific Heights Blvd.
San Diego, CA 92122
(800) 244-0575
http://www.jostenslearning.com

The Learning Company, Inc.
One Athenaeum St.
Cambridge, MA 02142
(800) 227-5609 or (617) 494-1200
Fax: (617) 494-1219
http://www.learningco.com

Learning 2000, Inc.
P. O. Box 831
Lawrenceburg, TN 38464
(888) 968-5327
Fax: (931) 852-3049
http://www.learning2000.com

LEXIS-NEXIS
3445 Newmark Dr.
P.O. Box 933
Dayton, OH 45401
(800) 262-2391 or (937) 865-6800
Fax: (937) 865-7305
http://www.lexis-nexis.com

Living Books
See Broderbund

Lotus Development Corp.
150 Cambridge Park Dr.
Cambridge, MA 02140
(800) 554-5501 or (617) 441-7000
Fax: (617) 441-7058

McAfee Associates, Inc.
2085 Bowers Ave.
Santa Clara, CA 95051-3832
(800) 332-9966 or (408) 988-3832
Fax: (408) 970-9727

MGX MacGraphics
1306 Houston St.
Austin, TX 78756
(512) 451-4298
Fax: (512) 450-1128
E-mail: info@
  mgxmacgraphics.com

Microsoft Corp.
One Microsoft Way
Redmond, WA 98052-6399
(800) 426-9400 or (800) 677-7377
Fax: (425) 936-7329
http://www.microsoft.com

Mindscape, Inc.
88 Rowland Way
Novato, CA 94945
(415) 895-2000
Fax: (415) 895-2102
http://www.mindscape.com

Motes Educational Software
P.O. Box 45294
Rio Rancho, NM 87174-5294

National Library of Medicine
see U.S. National Library
of Medicine

Netscape Communications Corp.
501 E. Middlefield Rd.
Mountain View, CA 94043
(800) 638-7483 or (650) 973-2555
Fax: (650) 937-2112
http://home.netscape.com

Newsbank, Inc.
58 Pine St.
New Canaan, CT 06840
(800) 243-7694
E-mail: Sales@newsbank.com
http://www.newsbank.com

OCLC, Inc.
6565 Frantz Rd.
Dublin, OH 43017-3395
(800) 848-5878
Fax: (614) 764-1640
http://www.nelinet.net

Outbound Train
(310) 378-7888
E-mail: sales@outboundtrain.com
http://www.outboundtrain.com

Outlook Software Corp.
13800 Montford Dr., Ste. 100
Dallas, TX 75240
(800) 925-5700 or (972) 774-0708
Fax: (972) 774-0689

Ovid Technologies, Inc.
333 Seventh Ave.
New York, NY 10001
(800) 950-2035
Fax: (212) 563-3784
E-mail: sales@ovid.com
http://www.ovid.com

Paul T. Dawson
P.O. Box 302
Ambler, PA 19002
http://archives.math.utk.edu/
  software/msdos/k-12/
  googol20/html

PolyBytes
3427 Bever Ave. SE
Cedar Rapids, IA 52403-3161
http://www.polybytes.com

Prentice-Hall New Media
1 Lake St., 5th Fl.
Upper Saddle River, NJ 07458
(800) 887-9998 or (201) 236-3459
Fax: (201) 236-7170

Public Information Kiosk, Inc.
20250 Century Blvd.
Germantown, MD 20874
(301) 916-1500
Fax: (301) 540-5522

Qdea
6331 Hilton Ct.
Pine Springs, MN 55115
(800) 933-0558 or (612) 779-0955
Fax: (612) 397-8590

QED Information Sciences, Inc.
170 Linden St.
P.O. Box 82-181
Wellesley, MA 02181
(617) 237-5656
Fax: (617) 235-0826

Qualcomm, Inc.
5775 Morehouse Dr.
San Diego, CA 92121
(858) 658-1121
Fax: (858) 658-2100
http://www.qualcomm.com

Quarterdeck
13160 Mindanao Way
Marina del Rey, CA 90202
(310) 309-3700
Fax: (310) 309-4219

Red Hat Software
79 T. W. Alexander Dr.
4201 Research Commons, Ste. 100
Research Triangle Park, NC 27709
http://www.redhat.com

Research Information Systems
Camino Corp. Center
2355 Camino Vida Roble
Carlsbad, CA 92009-1572
(800) 722-1227 or (760) 438-5526
Fax: (760) 438-5573

SilverPlatter Information Inc.
100 River Ridge Dr.
Norwood, MA 02062-5043
(800) 343-0064 or (781) 769-2599
Fax: (781) 769-8763
http://www.silverplatter.com

SIRS, Inc.
P.O. Box 2348
Boca Raton, FL 33427-2728
(800) 232-7477
Fax: (561) 994-4704
http://www.sirs.com

SmartStuff Software, Inc.
P.O. Box 82284
Portland, OR 97282
(800) 671-3999 or (503) 231-4300
Fax: (503) 231-4334
E-mail: info@smartstuff.com
http://www.smartstuff.com

Social Issues Resources Series, Inc.
P. O. Box 2348
Boca Raton, FL 33427-2348
(800) 232-7477 or (407) 994-4704
Fax: (407) 994-4704

Social Law Library
(617) 523-0018 x338
E-mail: pburns@socialaw.com
http://www.socialaw.com

SoftQuad, Inc.
20 Eglington Ave. W., 12th Fl.
P.O. Box 2025
Toronto, ON M4R 1K8 Canada
(800) 387-2777 or (416) 544-9000
Fax: (416) 544-0300
http://www.softquad.com

StarNine Technologies, Inc.
2550 Ninth St., Ste. 112
Berkeley, CA 94710
(800) 525-2580 or (510) 649-4949
Fax: (510) 548-0393

Sun Microsystems, Inc.
2550 Garcia Ave.
Mountain View, CA 94043-1100
(650) 960-1300
http://www.java.sun.com

Symantec Corp.
10201 Torre Ave.
Cupertino, CA 95014-2132
(800) 441-7234 or (800) 453-1193
Fax: (800) 554-4403
http://www.symantec.com

Tutorsystems
(800) 545-7766
Fax: (302) 631-1619
http://www.tutorsystems.com

U.S. National Library of Medicine
8600 Rockville Pike
Bethesda, MD 20894
(888) 346-3656
E-mail: publicinfo@nlm.nih.gov
http://www.nlm.nih.gov

ViaGrafix Corp.
One American Way
Pryor, OK 74361
(800) 842-4723 or (800) 233-3223
http://via1.viagrafix.com

Westlaw
(800) 344-5008
E-mail: store.webmaster@
  westgroup.com
http:www.westlaw.com

William S. Hein & Co., Inc.
1285 Main St.
Buffalo, NY 14209-1987
(800) 828-7571 or (716) 882-2600
Fax: (716) 883-8100
E-mail: mail@wshein.com
http://www.wshein.com

GLOSSARY

ASCII   (*A*merican *S*tandard *C*ode for *I*nformation *I*nterchange) A simplified, nearly universal code that all computers use to translate input from one to the other. It is particularly useful for the handling and exchange of text documents across different word processing programs.

Backup   A second or additional copy on a second disk of a program or data.

Bit   The smallest unit of information that a computer can process, either a *1* or a *0*. Bits are combined into groups of 8 or more to form a byte (computer word).

Bit-mapped graphics   Graphics are represented by an actual representation of the object (by *1*s and *0*s), rather than with a formula; the opposite of object-oriented graphics.

Boilerplate   Any text that is reused in various documents. It differs from a template, which is a blank form. In an office, boilerplate paragraphs or whole sections may be inserted into contracts, letters, and other documents, for example, a legal disclaimer that is used over and over.

Boolean logic   A technique that employs logic terms such as AND, OR, NOT to search a database.

Boot   The process of starting up a computer that prepares it for service. Usually, a small "bootstrap" program is loaded in automatically, making it possible to then load other programs. A cold boot is performed when the power to the unit is first turned on; a warm boot is performed if the machine is already on but needs to be reset.

Browser   Any of a variety of software packages that allow users to access the Internet (such as Netscape Navigator and Microsoft Internet Explorer).

Bulletin board system (BBS)   An electronic online messaging system. Many of these systems have been very elaborate and sophisticated. Much of the BBS effort was done on single, stand-alone PCs. This activity has been supplanted by the Internet.

Bundled   Software that comes with the hardware (for example, a word processor and a database management system) to make the system more marketable.

Byte Generally, 8 bits used during transmission, though stop and start bits may make it 10 bits. A byte is basically a computer word (character) such as *W* or *1*.

Cache A place where a computer stores information for speedier access.

CD-R (*C*ompact *D*isc–*R*ecordable) Recordable compact discs that can be written to. Some allow for multiple writes to the same disc. (*See also* CD-ROM.)

CD-ROM (*C*ompact *D*isc–*R*ead-*O*nly-*M*emory) A storage device that differs in several important ways from conventional disk drives. It will hold 650 megabytes of data and is more difficult to damage or erase than floppy disks. A major problem with CD-ROM is that data on it cannot be erased. The WORM (*W*rite *O*nce–*R*ead *M*any) and newer CD-ROMs are an effort to overcome this deficiency.

CD-ROM towers Devices that hold multiple CDs for use by a single computer or multiple computers across a LAN. They may operate as a host of CD-ROM drives or as CD changers. Towers are faster than a CD changer because a changer does not have a drive for every CD and must swap the CDs in and out as information on them is requested.

Central processing unit (CPU) The central brain or processor of the computer where timing, routing of data, and other decisions are made.

Client A workstation or microcomputer that is part of a client/server environment. A server computer may have many workstations connected to it that receive or exchange data with each client.

Clone A product that emulates a more-popular brand to capitalize upon its market.

CPU *See* Central processing unit.

Database A collection of data that is managed by a database management system or a file management system.

Database management system A computer program for storing and relating large amounts of information, such as credit cards, library cards, patron information, addresses, etc.

Dedicated A program, telephone line, or other device used for a single purpose or function.

Default Initial factory settings for hardware or software.

Desktop publishing Creating camera-ready copy with the computer and printer, often entailing a laser printer for high-quality production. Also refers to simpler products produced on a dot matrix printer with programs such as Print Shop.

Glossary **143**

Digital *1*s and *0*s that are added by the computer to form computer words or characters, as opposed to the analog or continuous signal of the telephone lines.

Disk A mass-storage device used in a disk drive to store and retrieve data.

Disk drive The mass-storage device that reads and writes to a disk. Such data-storage devices come in many sizes and types and may be built in or external to the computer.

Documentation The printed or online manuals that give instructions (help files) for using a program.

DOS (*D*isk *O*perating *S*ystem) The master control program that manages the computer's filing system and interfaces with the disk drives.

Download To receive a program or data into a computer from (usually) a computer in a remote location. It is the opposite of "upload." The "download" can then be copied to disk for future use.

DVD (*D*igital *V*ideo *D*isc) High capacity CD-ROM, useful for video and other multimedia applications.

E-mail (*E*lectronic *M*ail) Sending messages electronically. E-mail may be local through a bulletin board system, an Intranet, or through the global Internet.

Ergonomics The comfort (or lack thereof) provided in the workstation, including seating, lighting, and climate.

FAQ (*F*requently *A*sked *Q*uestions) A common help file seen on the Internet usually prepared by volunteer help. It contains basic information needed by new users to a service.

File manager A simple database system for organizing and handling one file of information at a time.

Font A complete set of letters, numerals, and symbols in a particular typeface or style.

Format To initialize a disk for use by the computer.

Freeware Software that has no copyright and that may be altered, given away, traded, or sold without any restrictions. (*See also* Shareware.)

Front End A client program for processing information at the user's end. It requests information or services from another computer or server.

FTP (*F*ile *T*ransfer *P*rotocol) The Internet service that transfers files over a TCP/IP network on the Internet. An FTP site act much like a warehouse, where large numbers of files may be stored for anyone to access, download, and use. They can be accessed anonymously or require a login and password, depending upon the owner.

Hard copy Printed computer data.

Hardware The nuts-and-bolts physical parts of the computer such as monitor, chips, keyboard, disk drives, etc.

Hertz Usually MegaHertz (MHz), a measurement of millions of cycles. The greater the Hertz, the faster the computer.

HTML (*H*yper*T*ext *M*arkup *L*anguage) A document format used to create and maintain Web pages with special codes that are embedded in the text.

HTTP (*H*yper*T*ext *T*ransfer *P*rotocol) The standard that defines how Web browsers communicate across the Web.

Integrated software Software packages that usually include word processing, database management, spreadsheet, telecommunications, and graphics.

Interactive Computer programs that require a human response. Noninteractive software (demo programs, for instance) will run without human intervention.

Internet The global network linking millions of computers. It consists of a set of protocols for exchanging information in many ways.

Intranet A term used to describe Web documents that have been placed on a local area network server for use within a company.

ISDN (*I*ntegrated *S*ervice *D*igital *N*etwork) A means of providing faster telecommunications. A computer may communicate at up to 128 K using ISDN.

JAVA A programming language created by Sun Microsystems for writing software for use on the Web. It is probably the most popular of the scripting languages available.

KB (*K*ilo*B*yte) 1,024 bytes of computer data.

LAN (*L*ocal *A*rea *N*etwork) A system that connects computers for the sharing of data, files, electronic mail, and peripherals.

Mainframe computer A large computer usually requiring air conditioning and a special room and support. The word "mainframe" refers to this support.

MB (*M*ega*B*yte) A disk storage unit of measure approximately 1 million bytes or 1,000 kilobytes of data.

Memory Where a computer stores and holds data. Data are stored short term in the computer's chips or, long term on hard or floppy disk drives.

MHz (*M*ega*H*ertz) The transmission speed of a computer measured in millions of cycles per second. The greater the MHz, the faster the CPU.

Modem   From the terms *mo*dulate/*dem*odulate; a device for translating the digital code of the computer into the analog code of the telephone line and back again. Two modems (one at each end) are required for two computers to communicate over the telephone. Computers can be directly connected without modems if they are close enough to connect with a cable.

Monitor   The screen that displays the computer's answers or data.

Mouse   Small, handheld device used to move the cursor on the screen as the device is moved about the desktop.

OPAC (*O*nline *P*ublic *A*ccess *C*atalog)   A computer-based library catalog for use by the public. It is accessed through a dumb terminal or PC. It replaces the card catalog.

Parity   An error-checking protocol for networking.

Peripheral   Any device that is not part of the computer proper, whether internal or external to the computer housing. Such devices include modems, printers, disk drives, scanners, and graphics tablets.

Printer   A device for printing out hard copy. Printers may be dot matrix, ink jet, or laser and may print in color or black and white.

Protocol   An agreed-upon method for data transmission that reduces the chance of error. For instance, if both computers know that all incoming sets of data bits or signals must add up to an even number, one coming in as an odd number is judged incorrect and must be transmitted again (see *Parity*). Other types include those on the Internet for ways of sending and receiving information.

Public domain software   Software without copyright restrictions.

RAM (*R*andom *A*ccess *M*emory)   Memory that is primary to a computer's functioning but is very transient. It is overwritten as data is processed.

ROM (*R*ead *O*nly *M*emory)   Memory in a computer that can be read but cannot be changed or added to.

Router   A hardware device that exchanges data between local and wide area networks. Routers used to be called *gateways* in some topologies.

Scanner   Device used to capture a photo or other hard copy image for use with computers by converting the image to a digital computer file.

Screen saver   A program that prevents burn-in, or static-image damage, on computer screens by keeping a moving pattern on the screen when a computer is not in use.

Search engine   A program used to search databases with specific terms or logic. Also, any of several hundred programs or indexes on the Internet that make it possible to find information quickly (for example, InfoSeek, Excite, etc.).

Server   Computer that acts as a hub for a network of workstations, either in a local area network or over the Internet.

Shareware   Copyrighted software that is freely distributed for demonstration purposes, but if the user wishes to continue to use it after an initial trial period, a license fee must be remitted to the owner of the software (stipulated in the software itself).

Software   The invisible part of the computer; the set of instructions that tells the hardware what to do with the data it receives.

Spell check   A program used to correct spelling and in some cases grammar.

Spreadsheet   The electronic version of the accountant's pad. Formulas and data may be entered and the results calculated immediately. A change in any data element will result in a recalculation of the entire spreadsheet, making it possible, for example, to judge the effect of changes in budgets very quickly.

Template   A form, electronic or paper, that represents work someone has prepared but that may be used over and over with different sets of data or information. An example would be the spreadsheet in which formulas have been placed for creating a budget.

Terminal   A place where people may interface with a computer through a keyboard, monitor, or printer. The computer (CPU or server) need not be present; it can be reached either through the telephone lines with a modem or directly through cable (known as hardwiring) in a local area network.

Trackballs   Assistive devices that are basically upside-down mice used to manipulate the computer for the same effect as a mouse by rolling a ball between the fingers instead of over a flat surface.

User group   Any group of people who exchange information about computers, especially problem solving. Such groups can host special events, such as having speakers or giving hardware/software demonstrations, or can get group discounts on computers and supplies.

VGA (*Video Graphics Array*)   A standard for graphics display developed by IBM. Today, it is considered minimum.

Video card   A special computer card with memory for producing a higher quality display.

Virus   A destructive program that replicates itself to cause mischief.

WAIS (*W*ide *A*rea *I*nformation *S*erver)   An Internet database that can be searched using the Z39.50 query language.

Web   *See* World Wide Web.

Word processing   A software program that allows users to rearrange and revise text (sentences, words, etc.) without having to retype everything before hard copy is produced. Often these programs come with "spell check" to check documents for suspect words (possibly misspelled words).

Word wrap   Most word processing programs use a word wrap feature to automatically wrap to the next line when typing to avoid repeated "carriage returns" (end-of-line hard returns).

Workstation   A work area equipped with furniture, outlets, data lines, computer hardware, table, etc. Such places should have good lighting and comfortable seating.

World Wide Web   The graphical protocol of the Internet. (*See also* HTML.)

WORM (*W*rite *O*nce–*R*ead *M*any)   A type of compact disc that allows for writing to disc but that cannot be erased. It can be read as often as desired.

Z39.50   A special protocol that allows online library catalogs to be searched across the Internet.

BIBLIOGRAPHY

Benson, Allen C., and Linda M. Fodemski. *Connecting Kids to the Internet: A Handbook for Librarians, Teachers, and Parents.* New York: Neal-Schuman, 1997.

Bern, Alan. "Access to the Internet in a Central Public Library Children's Room." *Youth Services in Libraries* (spring 1996): 253.

Bielefield, Arlene, and Lawrence Cheeseman. *Technology and the Copyright Law: A Guidebook for the Library, Research, and Teaching Professions.* New York: Neal-Schuman, 1997.

Brandt, D. Scott. "Compartmentalizing Computer Training." *Computers in Libraries* (Jan. 1998): 41.

Brooke, F. Dixon, Jr. "Subscription or Information Agency Services in the Electronic Era." *Serials Librarian* 29, no. 3/4 (1996): 57.

Boardman, Edna M. "How to Help Students Deal with 'Too Much Information.'" *The Book Report* (Sept./Oct. 1995): 23.

Caffarella, Edward P. "Planning for the Automation of School Library Media Centers." *Technology Trends* 41, no. 5 (1996): 33.

Cibbarelli, Pamela. "Windows NT Systems for Libraries: An Overview of Emerging Products." *Computers in Libraries* 17, no. 2 (Feb. 1997): 22.

Clyde, Laurel A. "Happy Anniversary, Computer Pals." *Emergency Librarian* 21 (Sept.-Oct. 1993): 57.

Commings, Karen. "Virtual Library Offers the Latest in Information Technology." *Computers in Libraries* 17, no. 2 (1997): 20.

Commings, Karen, Karen Cullings, and Connie Webster. "Community Information Goes Online in Central Pennsylvania." *Computers in Libraries* 15 (April 1995): 22.

Cunningham, Jim. "So You Want to Put Your Library on the Web?" *Computers in Libraries* 17, no. 2 (Feb. 1997): 42.

Dewey, Patrick R. *303 CD-ROMs to Use in Your Library: Descriptions, Evaluations, and Practical Advice.* Chicago: American Library Assn., 1995.

———. *303 Software Programs to Use in Your Library: Descriptions, Evaluations, and Practical Advice.* Chicago: American Library Assn., 1997.

Dittmer, Arlia. "Computer Tutors Puts Vets on the Net." *Illinois Libraries* 80, no. 1 (winter 1998): 32.

Dong, Xiaoying, and Louise T. Su. "Search Engines on the World Wide Web and Information Retrieval from the Internet: A Review and Evaluation." *Online & CD-ROM Review* 21, no. 2 (April 1997): 67.

Drumm, John E., and Frank M. Groom. "The Cybermobile: A Gateway for Public Access to Network-Based Information." *Computers in Libraries* 17 (Jan. 1997): 29.

Duvold, Ellen-Merete. "What is the Purpose of Project Activity in the Public Library Sector?" *Scandinavian Public Library Quarterly* 29, no. 3 (1996): 27.

Eisner, Joseph. "Disseminating Library-Produced Information by Direct Mail." *RQ* 34 (winter 1994): 150.

Ensor, Pat, ed. *The Cybrarian's Manual.* Chicago: American Library Assn., 1997.

Ford, Barbara J. "'All Together Now,' Make Your Point in *School Library Journal.*" *School Library Journal* 42, no. 4 (April 1996): 48.

Franklin, Patricia. "Opening a New Media Center in the Technology Age." *The Book Report* 14 (Sept./Oct. 1995): 20.

Glick, Andrea. "They Missed Mark Twain but Still Learned a Lot." *School Library Journal* 42, no. 12 (Dec. 1996): 13.

Gorman, Michael. "Ownership and Access: A New Idea of 'Collection.'" *College and Research Libraries News* 58, no. 7 (July/Aug. 1997): 498.

Holloway, Pat. "Buying a Computer for the Library." *Computers in Libraries* 14 (Jan. 1994): 30.

Holmes-Wong, Deborah, and others. "If You Build It, They Will Come: Spaces, Values and Services in the Digital Era." *Library Administration & Management* 11, no. 2 (spring 1997): 74.

Honey, Margaret. "Case Studies of K–12 Educators' Use of the Internet: Exploring the Relationship between Metaphor and Practice." *Ohio Media Spectrum* 47 (fall 1995): 24.

Hurt, Charlene. "Building Libraries in the Virtual Age." *College & Research Libraries News* 58, no. 2 (Feb. 1997): 75.

Jaffe, Lee David. *Introducing the Internet PLUS: A Model Presentation for Trainers.* 2d ed. Berkeley, Calif.: Library Solutions, 1996.

Jessop, Deborah. "A Survey of Recent Advances in Optical and Multimedia Information Technologies." *Computers in Libraries* 17, no. 2 (Feb. 1997): 53.

Jurist, Susan. "Creative Typography and Page Design for Libraries." *Library Software Review* 16, no. 2 (June 1997): 79.

Kesten, Philip R., and Slaven M. Zivkovic. "Electronic Reserves on the World Wide Web." *Journal of Interlibrary Loan, Document Delivery & Information Supply* 7, no. 4 (1997): 37.

Kohler, Stuart. "Contracting for computer services in libraries." *College & Research Libraries News* 58, no. 6 (June 1997): 399.

Lenzini, Rebecca T. "Delivery of Documents and More: A View of Trends Affecting Libraries and Publishers." *Journal of Library Administration* 22, no. 4 (1996): 49.

McCaffrey, Kate. "Technology Helper." *School Library Journal* 42 (Jan. 1996): 44.

McCarthy, Cheryl A., Sylvia C. Krausse, and Arthur A. Little. "Expectations and Effectiveness using CD-ROMs: What Do Patrons Want and How Satisfied Are They?" *College & Research Libraries News* 58, no. 2 (Feb. 1997): 128.

McCarthy, Connie Kearns. "Collection Development in the Access Age: All You Thought It Would Be and More!" *Journal of Library Administration* 22, no. 4 (1996): 15.

McKenzie, Barbara K., and others. "Trying to Reduce Your Technostress? Helpful Activities for Teachers and Library Media Specialists." *School Library Media Activities Monthly* 13, no. 9 (May 1997): 24.

Marmion, Dan. "LAN-Based Application Delivery." *Computers in Libraries* 17 (June 1997): 26.

Mather, Becky. "Surviving a Technology Whirlwind." *The Book Report* 14 (Sept./Oct. 1995): 18.

Maxymuk, John. *Using Desktop Publishing to Create Newsletters, Handouts, and Web Pages: A How-to-Do-It Manual.* New York: Neal-Schuman, 1997.

Mellon, Constance A. "Reflections on Technology, Books, and Children." *Youth Services in Libraries* 7 (winter 1994): 207.

Morgan, Eric Lease. "Computer Literacy for Librarians." *Computers in Libraries* 18 (Jan. 1998): 39.

Moyers, Michael. "Technology Column: What to Do with Those Old Computers." *New Jersey Libraries* 28 (fall 1995): 27.

Ogg, Harold C. *Introduction to the Use of Computers in Libraries: A Textbook for the Nontechnical Student.* Medford, N.J.: Information Today, 1997.

Ormes, Sarah, and Lorcan Dempsey, eds. *The Internet, Networking and the Public Library.* London, Eng.: Library Assn. Publishing, 1997.

Phillips, Carol Kolb. "Technology Column: Preschoolers and Computers in the Public Library: Perfect Together!" *New Jersey Libraries* 28 (summer 1995): 26.

Pipkin, Donald L. *Halting the Hacker: A Practical Guide to Computer Security.* Upper Saddle River, N.J.: Prentice-Hall, 1997.

Powers, Joan C. "CD-ROM in Schools: A Survey of Public Secondary Schools in Berkshire County, Massachusetts." *Reference Librarian* no. 49–50 (1995): 335.

Rhine, Leonard. "The Development of a Journal Evaluation Database Using Microsoft Access." *Serials Review* 22, no. 4 (winter 1996): 27.

Ross, Calvin. *The Frugal Youth Cybrarian: Bargain Computing for Kids.* Chicago: American Library Assn., 1997.

Safford, Barbara Ripp. "Transforming the Reference Collection: The Electric Library." *School Library Media Activities Monthly* 13, no. 7 (March 1997): 41.

Schuyler, Michael. "Computers and the Laze Factor." *Computers in Libraries* 17 (Feb. 1997): 26.

Scott, Jane. "Sneaking Literature into Technology Lessons." *School Library Media Activities Monthly* 12 (June 1996): 31.

Shreeves, Edward. "Is There a Future for Cooperative Collection Development in the Digital Age?" *Library Trends* 45, no. 3 (winter 1997): 373.

Stemmer, John K, and John Tombarge. "Building a Virtual Branch." *College & Research Libraries News* 58, no. 4 (April 1997): 244.

Will, Leonard, and Sheena Will. "Dewey for Windows." *The Electronic Library* 15, no. 3 (1997): 192.

Woodward, Jeannette. "Retraining the Profession; or, Over the Hill at 40." *American Libraries* 28, no. 4 (April 1997): 32.

York, Maurice C. "Value-Added Reference Service: The North Carolina Periodicals Index." *Computers in Libraries* 17 (May 1997): 30.

INDEX

A

A to Zap!, 19–20
Ablah Library, Wichita State University, 55, 58–9
Abonamah, Abdullah, 86–7
Accent Professional for Windows, 93–4
Adamowski, Mary, 20–1
Adamshick, Robert, 38–9
Adobe Acrobat, 92–3
Adobe PageMaker 6.5, 42–3, 49, 100–1
Adobe Pagemill, 92–3
Adobe Photo Deluxe, 107
Adobe Premiere, 92–3
Adventure, 16–17
Aggertt, Debra, 56–7
Ahern, Catherine, 101
Alpha 4 version 2.1, 80–1
Anastos, Sophia, 98–9
Anguilla Library, 16–17
Ann Arbor District Library, 85
Apache, 66–7, 67–9, 69–70
Apple Media Tool, 110–12
Apple QuickTime VR, 110–12
AppleShare, 29
Arlington Heights Memorial Library, 96
Armstrong, Ginger, 113–14
Ashland Public Library, 56–7
AskSam for Windows, 115
Association of Research Libraries, 7–8
Authorware, 97–8

B

B&T Link (Baker and Taylor), 80, 82–3
Bater, Richard, 9–10
Bell, Lori, 56–7
Benedicta, Sr., 28
Blixrud, Julia, 7–8
Blough–Weis Library, Susquehanna University, 25, 27
Blubaugh, Penny, 22–3
Box, Florence, 78–9
Brough, Susan, 107

C

C++, 86–7
Calcari, Susan, 67–9
Calumet City Public Library, 44
Career English, 96
Carlson, Sandy, 8–9
Carpenter Davies Associates, 35–6
Carpenter, Julie, 35–6
CBS Friesland, 35–6
Center of Excellence in Disaster Management & Humanitarian Assistance, Pacific Disaster Management Information Network Information Resource Center, 110–12
Centex WICAT, 34
Chesterfield County Public Library, 108, 113–14
Chicago Public Library, 54, 55, 56, 92
Chicago Tribune database, 74–6

Christian County Library, 45–6
Cinahl, 52–3
ClarisWorks, 101
Coastal Bend Health Information Network, 52–3
College of Medicine at Rockford, University of Illinois, 32
CollegeSource CD-ROM, 75–6
Columbia Library System, 26
Computer Assisted Legal Instruction (CALI), 31
Computer Sciences Department, University of Wisconsin–Madison, 66–7, 67–9, 69–70
Congressional Masterfile 1 and 2, 31
Conkis, Dixie, 114–15
Contemporary Authors, 23–4
Core Biomedical Collection, 52–3
Corel Classic Literature (CD-ROM), 75–6
Corel Draw, 92–3
Covington & Burling Library, 11
Crisp, Brandee, 70–1
Curious George, 21–2
Current Biography, 23
Cyber Patrol, 75–6

D

Dangerous Animals, 20
Dastur, Lee, 20
David S. Kitson Memorial Library, 99
deChambeau, Aimee, 86–7
Descriptive 2010, 96
Dewey, Patrick R., 6–7, 14–15, 72–3, 74–6, 82–3, 84, 117–18
Diskport Executive CD-ROM, 23–4
Dr. Seuss's ABCs, 21–2
Drewitt, David, 61–2
Dun's Million Dollar Disc, 116–17

E

EagleNet Resources, 31
Eisenhower Public Library, 16, 22–3, 48, 49
Eisner, Joseph, 42–3
Electric Library, 55, 73, 75–6
ELLIS Intro, 96
Emmanuel College Library, 97–8
Encyclopedia Americana, 23–4
English Vocabulary, 96
EOS International GLAS Series, 27–8
EOS International Managers Series 7.1, 25–6
Epic, 94–5
Essex Branch, Baltimore County Public Library, 95–6
Etter, Zana, 25–6
Eudora Pro E-Mail, 95–6
Euromonitor International, 116–17
Excite, 66–7, 67–9, 69–70
Exegy, 23–4

F

F & SA Index Plus, 116–17
Fichter, Darlene, 40–1, 50–1
FileMaker Pro, 31, 33, 66–7, 67–9, 69–70
Finkbeiner, Andrew, 23–4
FirstSearch, 23–4
Fitt, Chris, 107
Flanders, Kristin, 12
Focus on Grammar, 96
FoolProof Desktop Security, 76–7
Fortres, 23–4, 55, 101
Fox, Bruce, 17–18
FoxPro, 25, 29
Fun with a Purpose, 19–20

G

Garber, Marvin, 29
Geng, Zhong, 76–7

Gerber Hart Library and Archive, 26
Gibson, Sally, 52–3
Glenside Public Library District, 8, 83–4, 109
Goering, Bobbie, 88–9
Golden Book, 20
Golden Triangle Regional Library Consortium, 74, 78
Gonzaga University Library, 30–1
Googol Math Games, 16–17
Grant, Gaylia, 96–7
Grolier Multimedia Encyclopedia, 23–4
Gunderson, Gayle, 81–2
Guthrie, Lawrence S., II, 11

H

Hancock, Brian, 58–9
Harold Washington Library Center, Chicago Public Library, 55, 92, 99–101
Harvest Information Discovery and Access System 1.5.20, 58–9
Health Care Financing Administration database, 31
Health Reference Center, 52–3
HealthStar, 52–3
Hijack Pro 2.0, 94–5
Hodgkins Public Library, 114–15
Honsowitz, Aletha L., 41–2
HoTMetaL, 71–2, 114
Howell, J., 99
HTML Assistant Pro, 50–1, 63–4, 70–1
Human Body, 19–20

I

Ikiosk, 23–4
IMAP Mail Client, 31
Information Management Center, Baxter International, 108–9
InfoTrac database CD-ROM, 75–6
InfoTrac Search Bank, 23–4

J

J. Y. Joyner Library, 88, 89–90
JAVA, 86–7
JavaScript, 92–3
JFK Library, California State University, Los Angeles, Academic Technology Support, 32–3
John Toman Branch Library, Chicago Public Library, 33–4
Just Grandma and Me, 21–2

K

Kent County Library, 59–60
King County Library System, 38
Kitsap Regional Library, 6, 8–9
Kleckner, Larry, 106–7
Klinck Memorial Library, Concordia University, 12, 52, 53, 71
Kracke, Russell, 26
Krebsbach, Suzanne, 27–8
Krueger, Richard L., 59–60

L

La Grange Park Public Library, 108, 114–15
La Grange Public Library, 55, 114
Latham, Kevin, 36–7, 93–4, 103–4
LegalTrac, 31
Leibik, Lee, 48, 49
Lewis J. Ort Library, Frostburg State University, 101–3
LEXIS/NEXIS databases, 31, 33
Library Automation System, 78–9
Library Online Information Service (LOIS), 55, 61–2
Lifetime Library, 96
Linux 5.1, 58–9, 81–2
Living Books, 19–20
Lotus 1-2-3, 86
Lowe, Randall A., 101–3

M

McAfee VirusScan, 76–7, 101–3
MacGraphics Interface, 22–3
Magic School Bus, 19–20
Martin Memorial Library, 92, 105
Marywood University Library, 76–7
Massachusetts Administrative Law Library, 31
Master Pronunciation, 96
Masterplots, 23–4
Mavis Beacon Teaches Typing, 96, 99–101
Mavis Beacon Typing Tutor, 99–101
Maywood Public Library, 6–7, 14–15, 55, 72–3, 74–6, 82–3, 84, 108, 117–18
MEDLINE, 32, 52–3
Menu Builder, 23–4, 76–7
MGI, 107
Michigan State University Libraries, 92, 94–5
Microsoft Access, 25, 27, 33, 38, 97, 99–101, 108–9
Microsoft Encarta, 20
Microsoft Excel, 7–8, 31, 33, 38, 83–4, 85, 89–90, 95–6, 100–1
Microsoft FrontPage 98, 77–8, 112–13
Microsoft Index Server 2.0, 77–8
Microsoft Internet Explorer, 23–4, 33, 41–2, 63–4, 70–1, 73, 95–6, 97
Microsoft Internet Information Server 4.0, 77–8
Microsoft Office, 26, 77–8, 97, 100–1, 110–12
Microsoft Outlook, 33, 88–9
Microsoft PowerPoint, 31, 33, 38, 40–1, 78–9, 95–6, 100–1, 106–7
Microsoft Publisher, 17–18, 38, 99–101

Microsoft Windows, 16–17, 17–18, 19–20, 23–4, 28, 33, 38–9, 52–3, 71, 78–9, 83–4, 93–4, 97, 101–3, 110–12, 112–13, 116–17
Microsoft Windows for Workgroups 3.1, 8–9
Microsoft Windows NT Server 4.0 service pack 3, 77–8
Microsoft Word, 2, 5, 8–9, 17–18, 22–3, 25–6, 31, 33, 48, 49, 50–1, 58, 78–9, 80, 89–90, 93–4, 95–6, 99–101, 104, 109, 110
Microsoft Word HTML, 62–3
Microsoft Works, 6–7, 45–6, 93–4, 100–1
Microsoft Works File Manager, 28
Middle Mastery, 96
Miller, Kathleen M., 97
Millie's Math House, 19–20
Mishawaka-Penn Public Library, 46–7, 47–8, 80, 85–6
Mississippi State University, 74, 78
Mississippi University for Women, 74, 78
Montague Branch, Rockford Public Library, 19–20
Moskal, Steve, 55
Moulds, Michael, 8, 109
Munson, Kurt I., 53, 71
My First Amazing World Explorer, 19–20

N

National Library of Medicine databases, 32
Neal, Larry, 77–8
NELLICO Union Catalog, 31
Netherlands Centre for Libraries and Literature (NBLC), 35–6
Netscape Communicator, 4, 41–2, 63–4, 70–1, 97

Index

Netscape Navigator, 18–19, 20, 31, 33, 41–2, 55, 56, 58, 71, 75, 94–5, 97, 101–3
New Eagle Elementary Library, 20
Newsbank Databases CD-ROMs, 75–6
Niles Public Library District, 98–9
Northern Illinois University Libraries, 62–3, 80–1
Norton Utilities, 31
Novak, Vickie L., 44
NSA Library, Naples, Italy, 38–9
Nuremberg Trial Transcripts, 31
Nursing Collection, 52–3

O

OmniPage Pro, 50–1
Orland Park Public Library, 20–1
Ormes, Sarah, 71–2
Our Lady of Mount Carmel Parish, Carmel Prayer Center Library, 28
Ovid's Medical Collection, 52–3

P

Pagell, Ruth, 116–17
Paintbrush Pro, 71
Paintshop Pro, 40–1
Park Ridge Public Library, 49, 63–4, 70–1, 106–7
PC-File, 10, 47, 47–8
Perl scripts, freeware, 92–3
Peter Rabbit, 21–2
Phillips, Mabel G., 45–6
PI Kiosk, 59–60
Plainedge Public Library, 42–3
PolyView, 40–1
PolyView Screensaver, 40–1
Portage–Cragin Branch Library Computer Center, Chicago Public Library, 36–7, 92, 93–4, 103–4
Portsmouth Public Library, 106, 107
Presbyterian Church USA (Department of History), 6, 9–10
Print Shop, 40
ProCite for Windows, 13–14

Q

Quaterdeck Web Server 1, 62–3
Quattro Pro for Windows, 62–3
Queens Borough Public Library, 108, 109–10
QUEST, 31
QuickBooks, 26
Quicken, 12

R

Read for Meaning, 19–20
Reader's Guide, 23
Ready, Set, Go! 6.0, 44
Reed, Virginia R., 28
Rexx, 94–5
Ricoh Photostudio, 92–3
Ridgley, Katherine Neill, 112–13
Roanoke County Public Library System, 16, 18–19
Robert Wood Johnson Medical School, University of Medicine and Dentistry of New Jersey, 25–6
Rochester Hills Public Library, 74, 77–8
Rochester Regional Library Council, 97
Rockford Public Library, 23–4
Roden Branch, Chicago Public Library, 17–18
Rolsing, Kathy, 63–4
Russell Library, 101

S

Safe-Pay Connection, 84
Sage, Robert, 109–10
St. Joseph County Public Library, 54, 64–6
Sammy's Science House, 19–20

Santee Cooper Corporate Library, 27–8
School Mom, 16–17
Science and Technology Library, The University of Akron University Libraries, 86–7
Scottish Borders Council Library Service, 35–6
Seadle, Michael, 94–5
Seery, Mary Lou, 21–2
Sherrill, Charles A., 57–8
SilverPlatter databases, 33
SIRS Government Reporter CD-ROM, 23–4
SIRS Researcher, 23–4
Slader, Kathy, 95–6
Smith, Jim, 33–4
Smith, Lucy, 13–14
Smith, Nancy, 38
Smithsonian Institution, 112–13
Solock, Jack, 66–7
Spelman, Ivonne, 19–20
SPSS, 7–8
Starkville High School Library, 74, 78–9
Stephens, Jay, 18–19
Sulzer Regional Library, Chicago Public Library, 25, 29
Synchronize 1.3.02r, 81–2

T

Tennessee State Library and Archives, 57–8
Thomas M. Cooley Law School Library, 41–2
Tinley Park Public Library, 21–2
Titus, Elizabeth A., 62–3, 80–1
The Tortoise and the Hare, 21–2
Tricarico, Mary Ann, 97–8
Triton College Library/LRC, 13–14
Tucker, Dennis C., 46–7, 47–8, 85–6
Type!, 101
Typing Made Easy, 16–17

U

UK Office for Library and Information Networking, 71–2
Unicom Corporate Library, 88–9
United Nations Treaty Index, 30–1
University of Akron University Libraries, 80
University of North Carolina Law Library, 92–3
University of Saskatchewan Libraries, 40–1, 50–1
UVIEW, 31

V

Verge, Colleen, 85
Veria, Western Macedonia, Greece, public library, 35–6
ViaGrafix Training Videos, 98–9
VirusScan, 101–3
Vojtech, Kathryn, 83–4
Vreeland, Robert C., 92–3

W

Web browsers, 53
Web server software, 53
WebSTAR, 66–7, 67–9, 69–70
Weimar, Mary, 20–1
Wells, Amy Tracy, 69–70
WESTLAW databases, 31
Wichita State University Libraries, 81–2
Wilson, Rebecca A., 27
Winnie the Pooh and the Honey Tree, 21–2
WinSelect, 101–3
WinU, 101–3
Woodruff Library Center for Business Information, Emory University Libraries, 116–17
Worcestershire Libraries and Information Service, 61–2
WordPad, 48

WordPerfect, 2, 7, 11, 13, 14–15, 21, 25–6, 41–2, 75–6, 80, 100–1, 104, 108, 112–13, 117–18
WS_FTP, 50–1
Wyatt, Neal, 113–14

X
Xcmacs, 92–3

Y
Yackle, Anna, 49
York, Maurice C., 89–90

Z
Zastrow, Jan, 110–12

Patrick R. Dewey has been the Director of the Maywood Public Library District in Maywood, Illinois, since 1984. Prior to that he worked for the Chicago Public Library for ten years. His first job as a librarian was as editorial librarian for *Playboy Magazine*. He was also a columnist for two years for Wilson Library Bulletin, and an associate editor for *Computers in Libraries*. For nearly ten years he wrote reviews for *Booklist*. He has written twenty-five books, including six volumes of the American Library Association's 101 Micro Series. Other works include *Fan Club Directory* (McFarland), *National Directory of Bulletin Board Systems* (Meckler), *Essential Guide to Bulletin Board Systems* (Information Today), and *Public Access Microcomputers: A Handbook for Librarians* (G. K. Hall). He currently lives in Chicago with his dogs, Printer and Floppy. He may be reached at patrickdewey@hotmail.com.